M

PLANTS & GARDENS

BROOKLYN BOTANIC GARDEN RECORD

American Cottage Gardens

1990

Brooklyn Botanic Garden

Staff for this issue

RUTH ROHDE HASKELL, *Guest Editor*

BARBARA B. PESCH, *Editor*

CHARLES GABELER, *Art Director*

JANET MARINELLI, *Associate Editor*

and the Editorial Committee of the Brooklyn Botanic Garden

DONALD E. MOORE, *President, Brooklyn Botanic Garden*

ELIZABETH SCHOLTZ, *Director Emeritus*

STEPHEN K-M. TIM, *Vice President, Science & Publications*

PLANTS & GARDENS
BROOKLYN BOTANIC GARDEN RECORD

American Cottage Gardens

Vol. 46   Handbook #123   Spring 1990   No. 1

CONTENTS

Cover Photograph by Rob Procter, Procter-Macke garden

Plants and Gardens, Brooklyn Botanic Garden Record (ISSN 0362-5850) is published quarterly at 1000 Washington Ave., Brooklyn, N.Y. 11225, by the **Brooklyn Botanic Garden, Inc.** Second-class-postage paid at Brooklyn, N.Y., and at additional mailing offices. Subscriptions included in Botanic Garden membership dues ($20.00 per year), which includes newsletters and announcements. Copyright ©1990 by the Brooklyn Botanic Garden, Inc.
POSTMASTER: Send address changes to BROOKLYN BOTANIC GARDEN, Brooklyn, N.Y. 11225

foreword

In recent years, as Americans have become more interested in gardening, we've continued to look to England for information, inspiration and even plants. When most people think of a cottage garden, they imagine it surrounding a thatched Cotswold cottage, and England's cottage gardens do have much to offer. But America has its own cottage gardens, as indeed every country has, though seldom thatched cottages to go along with them. In America, the tradition of growing a few well-loved plants near the door goes back to colonial times. The dooryard gardens of New England, the flower gardens based on shared and traded plants in the South, the enclosed front yard gardens of Texas—these are *our* cottage gardens.

Historically, cottage gardens occupied the area in front of a modest dwelling and were fenced or hedged to keep out livestock. The cottagers didn't own the property but worked the land for someone else, and gardening was done in the precious time left over after work was finished. Archaic as it may sound, this scenario isn't relegated to the distant past. During my high school years my family lived in Colorado. On the highway a few miles from our home lived a rancher's hired hand and his family in a house provided by his employer. The tiny yard was fenced to protect it from straying animals, because cattle drives are a frequent summer occurrence on the highways. The hired man's wife, who I'm sure had her own ranch work to do, couldn't devote lots of time or space to gardening, but she grew lovely flowers in the front yard. I remember particularly the fragrant sweet peas growing up the wire fence. This isn't an isolated instance: Many families in those valleys today lead the same life.

There is a great deal of freedom in cottage gardening, which may be the primary reason it is so appealing. There is an element of chance. As plants are allowed to self-sow they seem to move about on their own (though usually under the gently guiding hand of the gardener), and the look of the garden changes subtly from year to year. This is not to suggest that a cottage garden is not arranged or designed, or that plants are put in without thought of how they will look with their neighbors. A haphazard mix of plants is usually a hodge-podge, and that's not a cottage garden—that's a mess.

Like a good Brunswick stew or clam chowder, there are a few essential ingredients in a cottage garden. It is often a mix of many types of plants —annuals, perennials, herbs, vines, shrubs, even vegetables—many of which may have been shared by friends and neighbors. These may be arranged according to the fancy of the gardener or as dictated by necessity, but the effect is intimate, personal, charming and casual. The result is a garden of cheerful atmosphere where the gardener can indulge a love of plants.

Ruth Rohde Haskell
Guest Editor

Ruth Rohde Haskell, guest editor of this handbook, was Associate Editor of Flower & Garden *for ten years. Her book on perennials will soon be published. She is now an associate editor for* Fine Gardening *magazine.*

A cottage garden is often a mix of many types of plants—annuals, perennials, herbs, vines, shrubs and even vegetables. Pictured here are one of grandmother's favorites—hollyhocks—marching in a line to the front door.

FRONT DOORYARDS

*"There are few of us who cannot
remember a front yard garden which
seemed to us a very paradise in
childhood. Whether the house was a
fine one and the enclosure spacious, or
whether it was a small house with
only a narrow bit of ground in front,
the yard was kept with care, and was
different from the rest of the land
altogether. . . . People do not know
what they lose when they make way
with the reserve, the separateness, the
sanctity, of the front yard of their
grandmothers. It is like writing down
family secrets for anyone to read; it is
like having everybody call you by
your first name, or sitting in any pew
in church."*

Country Byways
Sarah Orne Jewett, 1881

*A Garden at Ardmore, Pennsylvania circa
1910.*

Alice Morse Earle

Old New England villages and small
towns and well kept New England
farms had universally a simple and
pleasing form of garden called the front
yard or front dooryard. A few still may be
seen in conservative communities in the
New England states and in New York or
Pennsylvania. I saw flourishing ones this
summer in Gloucester, Marblehead and
Ipswich. Even where the front yard was
but a narrow strip of land before a tiny
cottage, it was carefully fenced in, with a
gate that was kept rigidly closed and

---

*Alice Morse Earle (1853–1911) was born in
Massachusetts, but moved to Brooklyn
Heights, NY after her marriage. Old Time
Gardens, a classic in American garden literature, is just one of a number of gardening
books she wrote. She is known to have cor-
responded with Gertrude Jekyll.*

latched. There seemed to be a law which
shaped and bounded the front yard; the
side fences extended from the corners of
the house to the front fence on the edge of
the road, and thus formed naturally the
guarded parallelogram. Often the fence
around the front yard was the only one on
the farm; everywhere else were boundaries
of great stone walls; or if there were rail
fences, the front yard fence was the only
painted one. I cannot doubt that the first
gardens that our foremothers had, which
were wholly of flowering plants, were
front yards, little enclosures hard won
from the forest.

The word yard, not generally applied
now to any enclosure of elegant cultivation, comes from the same root as the
word garden. Garth is another derivative
and the word exists much disguised in

orchard. In the 16th century yard was used in formal literature instead of garden; and later Burns writes of "Eden's bonnie yard, Where yeuthful lovers first were pair'd."

This front yard was an English fashion derived from the forecourt so strongly advised by Gervayse Markham (an interesting old English writer on floriculture and husbandry), and found in front of many a yeoman's house, and many a more pretentious house as well in Markham's day. Forecourts were common in England until the middle of the 18th century, and may still be seen. The forecourt gave privacy to the house even when in the centre of town. Its readoption is advised with handsome dwellings in England, where ground-space is limited—and why not America, too?

The front yard was sacred to the best beloved, or at any rate the most honored, garden flowers of the house mistress, and was preserved by its fences from inroads of cattle, which then wandered at their will and were not housed, or even enclosed at night. The flowers were often of scant variety, but were those deemed the gentlefolk of the flower world. There was a clump of daffodils and of the poet's narcissus in early spring, and stately crown imperial; usually, too, a few scarlet and yellow single tulips, and grape hyacinths. Later came phlox in abundance—the only native American plant—canterbury bells and ample and glowing London pride. Of course there were great plants of white and blue daylilies, with their beautiful and decorative leaves, and purple and yellow flower de luce. A few old-fashioned shrubs always were seen. By inflexible law there must be a lilac, which might be the aristocratic Persian lilac. A *Syringa*, flowering currant or strawberry bush made sweet the front yard in spring, and sent wafts of fragrance into the house-windows. Spindling, rusty snowberry bushes were by the gate, and snowballs also, or our native viburnums. Old as they seem, the spiraeas and deutzias came to us in the

19th century from Japan; as did the flowering quinces and cherries. The pink flowering almond dates back to the oldest front yards and Peter's wreath certainly seems an old settler and is found now in many front yards that remain.

The glory of the front yard was the old-fashioned early red "piny," cultivated since the days of Pliny. I hear people speaking of it with contempt as a derogatory adjective—but I glory in its flaunting. The modern varieties, of every tint from white through flesh color, coral, pink, ruby color, salmon and even yellow, to deep red, are as beautiful as roses. Some are sweet-scented; and they have no thorns, and their foliage is ever perfect, so I am sure the rose is jealous.

I am as fond of the peony as are the Chinese, among whom it is flower queen. It is by them regarded as an aristocratic flower; and in old New England towns fine peony plants in an old garden are pretty good indication of the residence of what Dr. Holmes called New England Brahmins. In Salem and Portsmouth are old "pinys" that have a hundred blossoms at a time—a glorious sight. A Japanese name is "flower-of-prosperity"; another name, "plant-of-twenty-days," because its glories last during that period of time.

Rhododendrons are to the modern garden what the peony was in the old-fashioned flower border; and I am glad the modern flower cannot drive the old one out. They are equally varied in coloring, but the peony is a much hardier plant, and I like it far better. It has no blights, no bugs, no diseases, no running out, no funguses; it doesn't have to be covered in winter and it will bloom in the shade. No old-time or modern garden is to me fully furnished without peonies. I would grow them in some corner of the garden for their splendid healthy foliage if they hadn't a blossom. The *Paeonia tenuifolia* in particular has exquisite feathery foliage. The great tree peony, which came from China, grows eight feet or more in height,

A Garden at Bar Harbor, Maine.

is described as set around with gillyflower, tansy, gromwell and "pyonys powdered ay betwene"—just as I like to see peonies set to this day, "powdered" everywhere between the other flowers of the border.

I am pleased to note of the common flowers of the New England front yard, that they are no new things; they are nearly all Elizabethan of date—many are older still. Lord Bacon in his essay on gardens names many of them, crocus, tulip, hyacinth, daffodil, flower de luce, double peony, lilac, lily of the valley.

A favorite flower was the yellow garden lily, the lemon lily, *Hemerocallis*, when it could be kept from spreading. Often its unbounded luxuriance exiled it from the front yard to the kitchen dooryard. Its pretty old-fashioned name was liriconfancy, given, I am told, in England to the lily of the valley. I know no more satisfying sight than a good bank of these lemon lilies in full flower.

The time of fullest inflorescence of the 19th century front yard was when phlox and tiger lilies bloomed; but the pinkish-orange colors of the latter (the oddest reds of any flower tints) blended most vilely and rampantly with the crimson-purple of the phlox; and when London pride joined with its glowing scarlet, the front yard fairly ached. Nevertheless, an adaptation of that front-yard bloom can be most effective in a garden border, when white phlox only is planted, and the tiger lily or cultivated stalks of our wild nodding lily rise above the white trusses of bloom. These wild lilies grow very luxuriantly in the garden, often towering above our heads and forming great candelabra bearing two score or more blooms. It is no easy task to secure their deep-rooted rhizomes in the meadow. I know a young man who won his sweetheart by the patience and assiduity with which he dug for her all one broiling morning to secure for her the coveted lily roots, and col-

and is a triumph of the flower world; but was not known in the oldest front yards. Some of the tree peonies have finely displayed leafage of a curious and very gratifying tint of green. Miss Jekyll, with her usual felicity, compares its blue cast with pinkish shading to the vari-colored metal alloys of the Japanese bronze workers—a striking comparison. The single peonies of recent years are of great beauty, and will soon be esteemed here as in China.

Not the least of the peony's charms is its exceeding trimness and cleanliness. The plants always look like a well dressed, well shod, well gloved girl of birth, breeding and of equal good taste and good health; a girl who can swim, and skate, and ride and play golf. Every inch has a well set, neat, cared-for look which the shape and growth of the plant keeps from seeming artificial or finicky.

No flower can be set in our garden of more distinct antiquity than the peony; the Greeks believed it to be of divine origin. A green arbor of the 14th century in England lapsed with mild sunstroke at the finish. Her gratitude and remorse were equal factors in his favor.

The tiger lily is usually thought upon as a truly old-fashioned flower, a veritable antique; it is a favorite of artists to place as an accessory in their colonial gardens, and of authors for their flower-beds of Revolutionary days, but was not known either in formal garden or front yard until after "the days when we lived under the King." The bulbs were first brought to England from Eastern Asia in 1804 by Captain Kirkpatrick of the East India Company's Service, and shared with the Japan lily the honor of being the first Eastern Lilies introduced into European gardens. A few years ago an old gentleman, Mr. Isaac Pitman, who was then about 85 years of age, told me that he recalled distinctly when tiger lilies first appeared in our gardens, and where he first saw them growing in Boston. So instead of being an

This old illustration shows a combination of rose loosestrife, white mullein, mullein pinks and yellow knapweed. The colors blend nicely.

old-time flower, or even an old-comer from the Orient, it is one of the novelties of this century. How readily has it made itself at home, and even wandered wild down our roadsides!

The two simple colors of phlox of the old-time front yard, white and crimson-purple, are now augmented by tints of salmon, vermilion and rose. I recall with special pleasure the profuse garden decoration at East Hampton, Long Island, of a pure cherry-colored phlox, generally a doubtful color to me, but there so associated with the white blooms of various other plants, and backed by a high hedge covered solidly with blossoming honeysuckle, that it was wonderfully successful.

To other members of the phlox family, all natives of our own continent, the old front yard owed much; the moss pink sometimes crowded out both grass and its companion the periwinkle; it is still found in our gardens, and bountifully also in our fields; either in white or pink, it is one of the satisfactions of spring, and its cheerful little blossom is of wonderful use in many waste places. An old-fashioned bloom, the low-growing *Phlox amoena*, with its queerly fuzzy leaves and bright crimson blossoms, was among the most distinctly old-fashioned flowers of the front yard. It was tolerated rather than cultivated, as was its companion, the *Arabis* or rock cress—both crowding, monopolizing creatures. I remember well how they spread over the beds and up the grass banks in my mother's garden, how sternly they were uprooted, in spite of the pretty name of the *Arabis*—"snow in summer."

Sometimes the front yard path had edgings of sweet single or lightly double white or tinted pinks, which were not deemed as choice as box edgings. Frequently large box plants clipped into simple and natural shapes stood at the side of the doorstep, usually in the homes of the well-to-do. A great shell might be on either side of the doorsill, if there chanced to be seafaring men-folk who lived or visited under the roof-tree. Annuals were few in number; sturdy old perennial plants of many years' growth were the most honored dwellers in the front yard, true representatives of old families. The roses were few and poor, for there was usually some great tree just without the gate, an elm or larch, whose shadow fell far too near and heavily for the health of roses. Sometimes there was a prickly semidouble yellow rose, called by us a Scotch rose, a sweet brier or a rusty-flowered white rose, similar, though inferior, to the Madame Plantier. A new fashion of trellises appeared in the front yard about 60 years ago, and crimson Boursault roses climbed up them as if by magic.

One marked characteristic of the front yard was its lack of weeds; few sprung up, none came to seed-time; the enclosure was small, and it was a mark of good breeding to care for it well. Sometimes, however, the earth was covered closely under shrubs and plants with the cheerful little ladies' delights, and they blossomed in the chinks of the bricked path and under the box edges. Ambrosia, too, grew everywhere, but these were welcome—they were not weeds.

Our old New England houses were suited in color and outline to their front yards as to our landscape. Lowell has given in verse a good description of the kind of New England house that always had a front dooryard of flowers.

"On a grass-green swell
That towards the south with sweet
concessions fell,
It dwelt retired, and half had grown to be
As aboriginal as rock or tree.
It nestled close to earth, and seemed to brood
O'er homely thoughts in a half-conscious
mood.
If paint it e'er had known, it knew no more
Than yellow lichens spattered thickly o'er
That soft lead gray, less dark beneath the
eaves

Which the slow brush of wind and weather
leaves
The ample roof sloped backward to the
ground
And vassal lean-tos gathered thickly
round,
Patched on, as sire or son had felt the need.
But the great chimney was the central
thought.
It rose broad-shouldered, kindly, debonair,
Its warm breath whitening in the autumn
air."

Sarah Orne Jewett, in the plaint of *A Mournful Villager*, had drawn a beautiful and sympathetic picture of these front yards, and she deplores their passing. I mourn them as I do every fenced-in or hedged-in garden enclosure. The sanctity and reserve of these front yards of our grandmothers was somewhat emblematic of woman's life of that day: it was restricted, and narrowed to a small outlook and monotonous likeness to her neighbor's; but it was a life easily satisfied with small pleasures, and it was comely and sheltered and carefully kept, and pleasant to the home household; and these were no mean things.

The front yard was never a garden of pleasure; children could not play in these precious little enclosed plots, and never could pick the flowers—front yard and flowers were both too much respected. Only formal visitors entered therein, visitors who opened the gate and closed it carefully behind them, and knocked slowly with the brass knocker, and were ushered in through the ceremonious front door and the little ill-contrived entry, to the stiff foreroom or parlor. The parson and his wife entered that portal, and sometimes a solemn would-be sweetheart, or the guests at a tea party. It can be seen that everyone who had enough social dignity to have a front door and had a parlor, and visitors thereto, also desired a front yard with flowers as the external token of that honored standing. It was like owning a pew in church; you could be a Christian without having a pew, but not a respected one. Sometimes when there was a "vendue" in the house, reckless folk opened the front gate, and even tied it back. I attended one where the auctioneer boldly set the articles out through the windows under the lilac bushes and even on the precious front yard plants. A vendue and a funeral were the only gatherings in country communities when the entire neighborhood came freely to an old homestead, when all were at liberty to enter the front dooryard. At the sad time when a funeral took place in the house, the front gate was fastened widely open, and solemn men-neighbors, in Sunday garments, stood rather uncomfortably and awkwardly around the front yard as the women passed into the house of mourning and were seated within. When the sad services began, the men too entered and stood stiffly by the door. Then through the front door, down the mossy path of the front yard and through the open front gate was borne the master, the mistress, and then their children, and children's children. All are gone from our sight, many from our memory, and often too from our ken, while the lilacs and peonies and flowers de luce still blossom and flourish with perennial youth, and still claim us as friends.

At the side of the house or by the kitchen door would be seen many thrifty blooms: poles of scarlet runners, beds of portulacas and petunias, rows of pinks, bunches of marigolds, level expanses of sweet williams, banks of cheerful nasturtiums, tangles of morning-glories and long rows of stately hollyhocks, which were much admired, but were seldom seen in the front yard, which was too shaded for them. Weeds grew here at the kitchen door in a rank profusion which was hard to conquer; but here the winter's fuchsias or geraniums stood in flower pots in the sunlight, and the tubs of oleanders and agapanthus lilies.

The flowers of the front yard seemed to bear a more formal, a "company" aspect; conventionality rigidly bound them. Bachelor's buttons might grow there by accident, but marigolds never were tolerated—they were pot herbs. Sunflowers were not even permitted in the flower beds at the side of house unless these stretched down to the vegetable beds. Outside the front yard would be a rioting and cheerful growth of pink bouncing bet, or of purple honesty, and tall straggling plants of a certain small flowered, ragged *Campanula,* and a white mallow with flannelly leaves which, doubtless, aspired to inhabit the sacred bounds of the front yard (and probably dwelt there originally), and often were gladly permitted to grow in side gardens or kitchen dooryards, but which were regarded as interloping weeds by the guardians of the front yard, and sternly exiled. Sometimes a bed of these orange-tawny daylilies which had once been warmly welcomed from the Orient, and now were not wanted anywhere by anyone, kept company with the bouncing bet, and stretched cheerfully down the roadside.

When the fences disappeared with the night rambles of the cows, the front yards gradually changed character; the tender blooms vanished, but the tall shrubs and the peonies and flower de luce sturdily grew and blossomed, save where that dreary destroyer of a garden crept in—the desire for a lawn. The result was then a meagre expanse of poorly kept grass, with no variety, color or change—neither lawn nor front yard. It is ever a pleasure to me when driving in a village street or a country road to find one of these front yards still enclosed, or even to note in front of many houses the traces of a past front yard still plainly visible in the flourishing old-fashioned plants of many years' growth. ❀

Excerpted from Alice Morse Earle's Old-Time Gardens, *1901.*

Herbs in a
SMALL CITY GARDEN

Virginia & Sarah Weatherly

Growing herbs with our perennials— in fact, mixing all our plants including shrubbery—has become so natural that we have forgotten that at one time we had customary perennial, cutting, herb and vegetable gardens. When we moved from family property with large gardens to a pocket-size city lot, we had many changes to consider.

First was the size, as the house and grounds were only 75 feet by 150 feet. Unbelievable as it seems there were 13 huge trees on this small space—mostly American elms. Even though three trees were removed, there was very little sunlight. Shade gardening was a new experience for us. Our mother, a knowledgeable and self-taught horticulturist, set to work researching shade-loving plants and recording data on sunlight in various parts of the property. During a rainstorm it was

Having so little space, the authors realized that every square inch had to be cultivated if they were to enjoy some of the plants that they wanted to grow. Pictured here is crape-myrtle walk.

Grass walk ends with an inviting bench—a place to sit and enjoy the garden and watch the birds that come to the feeders. Many of the plants in the garden are fragrant so that the gentle breezes waft the mingled scents.

not unusual to see her walking around the garden under an umbrella diagraming the flow of the water. All of this resulted in placing essential plants in spots where they would have a reasonable chance of survival. It was surprising that this mixture of plants could evolve into a fairly artistic and homogeneous garden.

Having so little ground, we finally realized that every square inch must be cultivated if we were to enjoy some of the plants that we felt were indispensable. Mother designed patterned beds into small gardens, giving each of them names.

Virginia and Sarah Weatherly have been gardening the same plot in Kansas City for 45 years. They keep extensive records which include the source of each plant and the date it was planted.

The Sweet Herb Garden has 12 small beds joined by a partially bricked path covered with creeping thyme. Two very small beds are filled with *Nepeta mussinii*. Two more are planted with *Dictamnus alba*. An ideal spot was found here for French tarragon. Pink, blue and white hyssop edged one side while black (now red) raspberry canes climb the fence on another side. The texture of tough herbs like costmary and rue blend well and fill large and more difficult spots. Throughout this garden species bulbs are planted for early spring bloom, succeeded by hardy lilies and then *Allium tanguticum*. One of the criteria is fragrance. In the early shady garden days, color was at a premium, so sweet william (*Dianthus barbatus*) 'Newport Pink' was very welcome. Yarrow blooms all summer, as do coralbells. Dianthuses cover any bare ground along with a wonderful johnny-jump-up, *Viola tricolor* 'Black Imp', which self-sows.

To our great joy two peony and hybrid rose beds could become our vegetable garden after the Dutch Elm disease destroyed all the elms. Naturally some of the annual culinary herbs are placed here. Climbing nasturtiums usually make a background for these vegetables. Throughout this area dill self-sows and as it is so pretty, it is allowed to remain until it interferes with other plants.

Our Grass Walk is on the western edge of the property. Originally only deep shade-loving plants could survive, such as hostas and ferns. Now there are five fruit trees, peonies, two old roses ('Gruss an Aachen' and 'Old Blush'), anemones (*A. japonica, sylvestris, vitifolia*), *Physostegia*, meadowrue (*Thalictrum*) and the original plants—celandine, bergamot, *Colchicum autumnale*, sweet woodruff, *Daphne cneorum* and *D. burkwoodii*, wild sweet william (*Phlox divaricata*), various ferns and ground covers (lamiums, sweet woodruff and epimediums) enjoy the additional sun. These, with six Exbury azaleas, a yew, two small hollies, climbing clematis on the board fence and a hydrangea have become very happy companions even though a sawtooth oak tree is rapidly growing to gigantic proportions.

Moving eastward on the property, we always had more morning sun and so could have color. A hedge of old roses (moss, damask, cabbage and hybrid musk) screen this side. This is underplanted with wildflowers and ground covers (wild ginger and grandiflora primroses). Aruncus does well here.

This area is the background for our perennial garden, which is six raised beds. The focal point is a small circular bed with a lead figure of St. Francis surrounded by 'Hidcote' and 'Munstead' lavender. These plants seed in the sand of the brick paths and over the years we have been able to edge two sides of each of three beds. The other sides are edged with Korean box which were rooted trimmings from the hedge in front. There are many bulbs in the spring, and they, with *Ribes aureum* (Missouri currant), provide wonderful early fragrance. The continuous bloom comes from *Lythrum* 'Morden's Pink', *Thalictrum glaucum*, yarrow (*Achillea taygetea*), *Veronica* 'Minuet' and *V. spicata* 'Red Fox', phlox, *Digitalis* (foxglove), valerian (*Centranthus ruber*), *Clematis integrifolia* and *C. recta*, many varieties of alliums, *Aster frikartii*, *Delphinium* x *belladonna* and hybrid lilies.

Two narrow rectangular beds are on either side of the above four. The one with the least sun contains garden sage, variegated sage, coreopsis, *Amsonia*, *Stokesia*, *Santolina virens* and *S. chamaecyparissus*, *Veronica prostrata* 'Heavenly Blue' and *Scabiosa*. Throughout the garden many varieties and colors of dianthus and sweet william are scattered where there is a bare square inch.

The sixth bed is for culinary herbs. This is the only section that is not a mixture. As this bed is the foreground to the perennial gardens seen from the brick terrace, the basils, chives, thymes, lovage, rosemary, pineapple sage, fern-leaf tansy, oregano, salad burnet, winter and summer savories, sorrel, parsleys and sweet marjoram make a nice contrast of greens.

The beds edging the brick terrace and front porch also have some herbs. Lady's-mantle (*Alchemilla*), *Helleborus orientalis*, clary sage, Jacob's ladder (*Polemonium*) and sweet cicely are happy under *Calycanthus*, dwarf crape-myrtle and *Exochorda* 'The Bride'.

In containers on the terrace, we have lemon verbena, many scented-leaved geraniums, tender ivies and sweet bay (*Laurus nobilis*).

Throughout the property white nicotiana and feverfew self-sow and are allowed to stay if they do not crowd out another plant.

We realized very early that we did not have enough space for some weedy but fragrant herbs, so we went outside to the parking area with these. Here we could let bronze fennel, lemon balm, *Artemisia ludoviciana* 'Silver King', many mints and common tansy spread to their hearts' content. This planting is very popular with the joggers.

As many herbs are spreaders, caution must be used in combining them with perennials and shrubbery. What started as a necessity for us has now become a way of gardening, and we recommend using all plants in any spot that will artistically or horticulturally please you. ❀

Plant List

Herbs:

Artemisia ludoviciana 'Silver King'	
Basil	*Ocimum basilicum*
Bergamot	*Monarda didyma*
Wood Betony	*Stachys officinalis*
Catmint	*Nepeta mussinii*
Celandine	*Chelidonium majus*
Chives	*Allium schoenoprasum*
Chervil	*Anthriscus cerefolium*
Costmary	*Chrysanthemum balsamita*
Dill	*Anethum graveolens*
Feverfew	*Chrysanthemum parthenium*
Germander	*Teucrium chamaedrys*
Heartsease	*Viola* x *wittrockiana*
Horehound	*Marrubium vulgare*
Jacob's-ladder	*Polemonium caeruleum*
Lady's-mantle	*Alchemilla vulgaris*
Lavender	*Lavandula officinalis*
Lemon balm	*Melissa officinalis*
Lemon verbena	*Aloysia triphylla*
Lovage	*Levisticum officinale*
Pot Marigold	*Calendula officinalis*
Marjoram	*Origanum marjorana*
Mint	*Mentha piperita, spicata, rotundifolia*
Nasturtium	*Tropaeolum majus*
Nicotiana spp.	
Oregano	*Origanum vulgare*
Orris root	*Iris* x *germanica*
Parsley	*Petroselinum crispum*
Periwinkle	*Vinca minor*
Rosemary	*Rosmarinus officinalis*
Rue	*Ruta graveolens*
Sages	*Salvia officinalis, S. pratensis* (clary), *S. elegans* (pineapple)
Salad burnet	*Poterium sanguisorba*
Santolinas	*Santolina virens* (green), *S. chamaecyparissus* (lavender cotton, gray)
Savory	*Satureja hortensis* (summer), *S. montana* (winter)
Scented-leaf geraniums	*Pelargonium* spp.
Sorrel, French	*Rumex scutatus*
Sweet bay	*Laurus nobilis*
Sweet Cicely	*Myrrhis odorata*
Tansy	*Tanacetum vulgare, T. vulgare crispum* (fern-leaf tansy)
Tarragon, French	*Artemisia dracunculus*
Thyme	*Thymus vulgaris* (common), *T. serpyllum* cvs., *T.* x *citriodorus* (lemon)

Valerian	*Centranthus ruber*
Sweet woodruff	*Galium odoratum*
Yarrow	*Achillea taygetea*

Poisonous Drug Herbs:

Meadow saffron	*Colchicum autumnale*
Foxglove	*Digitalis* spp.
Guinea-hen flower	*Fritillaria meleagris*
Lenten rose	*Helleborus orientalis*

Scented and Aromatic Shrubs:

Carolina allspice	*Calycanthus floridus*
Blue mist	*Caryopteris* x *clandonensis*
Daphne cneorum and *D. burkwoodii*	
Witch hazel	*Hamamelis virginiana*
Honeysuckle	*Lonicera heckrottii*
Mock-orange	*Philadelphus* spp.
Missouri currant	*Ribes aureum*
Viburnum carlesii	

A large sweet bay tree occupies a large tub on the terrace. The beds edging this area have herbs, lady's mantle, clary sage, jacob's ladder, sweet cicely, crape-myrtle and lenten rose.

Antique Plants for
MODERN COTTAGE GARDENS

Arthur O. Tucker

I f cottage gardening could be distilled to an essence, it would include an exuberance of growth, color and scent. This style of gardening was originally dictated by the plants themselves. While the cottage garden revival often includes the classic vision of an English thatched cottage, the vernacular gardens of our North American ancestors were essentially cottage gardens, and their plants are perfect for this style.

Above: *A cottage garden borders the walkway leading to the house and contains showy foxgloves and* Achillea 'Moonshine'.

Top Right: *Foxgloves are combined with roses,* Lysimachia ciliata *(left rear) and* Silene dioica *'Flore Pleno' which dates to pre-1581.*

Right: *'New Dawn' roses of the 1930s envelop this archway. Planted at the base are lavender cotton and lamb's ears.*

Arthur O. Tucker is a Research Professor in the Department of Agriculture and Natural Resources at Delaware State College in Dover, Delaware. He has published on the systematics, chemistry and agronomic management of herbs and essential oil plants, but his private passion is saving antique cultivars of ornamental plants.

Ironically, the best source of antique plants for cottage gardens is consistently ignored: neighborhood gardens. Common plants quickly become considered vulgar and are often ignored by "sophisticated" gardeners who demand the latest cultivars described in glowing terms in the catalogs. Elizabeth Lawrence was one of the first Americans to write of the treasures in our own backyards that are, as a bonus, regionally adapted.

A good example is grandmother's early blue iris (*Iris germanica*). With blue standards and purple-blue falls, this is probably the very first intermediate tall bearded iris to bloom in neighborhood gardens of the northeastern U.S. It probably dates back to the ninth century A.D., and was a subject of Van Gogh's floral paintings in 1889. 'Honorabile' (1840), a miniature tall bearded with yellow standards and yellow falls solidly veined with maroon-red, is another very common iris of our old gardens. Gradually, specialty iris nurseries are again offering antique irises, and HIPS (Historic Iris Preservation Society) further acts to preserve these treasures. While modern irises flaunt their superb beauty, they demand to be used as accent plants or planted *en masse* with other irises, but the old irises blend beautifully into a perennial border.

Perhaps no flowers are more characteristic of cottage gardens of North America than the old roses. Again, dooryard gardens show regional adaptability, with old teas and noisettes in the southeastern U.S. and hybrid provences and hybrid chinas in the northeastern states. 'Banshee' (c. 1773), probably a hybrid of *R. damascena* and *R. blanda*, exists in up to nine different forms scattered across North America! 'Bella Donna' (pre-1829), 'Pink Leda' (c. 1840), and 'Shailer's Provence' (1799) are only occasionally available at specialty nurseries, yet cloak the graveyards and farmyard gardens throughout the mid-Atlantic region. On their own roots these all suck-

IRIS GERMANICA.

er, and their widespread distribution alludes to frequent passes over the back fence. Thanks to the Heritage Rose Group, these roses of our ancestral gardens are being preserved. Join these specialty groups to learn more and perhaps acquire plants!

The American gardener was, in years past, the recipient of the fruits of the English "florist," or one who devoted himself to the breeding of one particular flower. *Dianthus* and *Primula* are only two genera of such florist flowers. Derivatives of the cottage pink (*D. plumarius*), clove pink (*D. caryophyllus*), and their hybrids are often found in old American gardens. 'Gloriosa' (late 18th century), a sumptuous pink/carnation hybrid full of clove fragrance, was found growing in a garden in Seattle. The most common primulas in American gardens are variants of the old brick-red polyanhus (*P.* x *polyantha*), which date back to at least the 17th century and seem resistant to the heat and humidity of an American summer (unlike their hybrid derivatives, the 'Pacific Giants'). The old sulfur yellow, a selection of *P.* x *media,* is also characteristic of neighborhood gardens of the U.S. and dates back to before 1601.

Daylilies, daffodils and peonies are appropriate to a cottage garden and persist in our gardens long after the old traces of man decay around them. The most common daylily of our roadsides is a sterile clone, *Hemerocallis fulva* 'Europa', which must be propagated vegetatively; it dates from before 1567. The double fulvous-orange daylily may be found as either the green reversion of 'Kwanso' (introduced with variegated foliage in 1864 but reverted to all green by 1917), or 'Flore Pleno' (1860). While I have often heard that gardeners have the true lemon lily (*H. lilioasphodelus*, formerly *H. flava*, of 1570), invariably it turns out to be 'Hyperion', introduced in 1925. The most common daffodil of our old gardens in the U.S. has earned the colloquial name of 'Butter and Eggs', but is more correctly called 'Telamonius Plenus' or 'Van Sion'. This sloppy double yellow daffodil, often bearing streaks of green, was listed by Parkinson in 1629 as "Mr. Wilmer's great double daffodill." If you order this daffodil from commercial sources, you inevitably receive 'Plenus', which is just as old but usually bears only a double cup, though sometimes the doubling extends to the entire perianth. Another common daffodil is 'Primrose Peerless', which was also mentioned by Parkinson; it bears a pale yellow cup against white perianth segments, usually with two flowers per scape. The antique peonies in our old gardens are almost impossible to identify, but the old red piney ('Rosea Plena') of pre-1597 and the fern-leaved peony (*Paeonia tenuifolia* 'Plena') of 1765 are some to treasure. Peony nurseries also offer old cultivars such as 'Avalanche' (1886), 'Edulis Superba' (1824), 'Felix Crousse' (1881), 'Festiva Maxima' (1851), 'Grover Cleveland' (1904), 'Karl Rosenfeld' (1908), 'Mikado' (1893), 'M. Jules Elie' (1888) and 'Sarah Bernhardt' (1906).

Don't neglect the vines, so essential for a touch of romanticism in a cottage garden. Wisteria and Hall's Japanese honeysuckle (*Lonicera japonica* 'Halliana') abound in our old gardens. A real treasure is the hardy fragrant jasmine, *Jasminum officinale*. A painting of William Bartram by Charles Wilson Peale, done in 1808, shows this jasmine, which is hardy to Philadelphia. Many old cultivars of English ivy (*Hedera helix*) seem to be perfectly hardy to at least Zone 6. Choose such ivies as 'Atropurpurea' (1882), 'Conglomerata' (1871), 'Dealbata' (1872), 'Deltoidea' (1871), 'Sulphurea' (1872) or 'Tricolor' (1860).

Window boxes and pots of antique house plants round out the picture. *Pelargonium inquinans*, the first geranium brought to the U.S., was painted by Rubens Peale in 1801, while the variegated, non-flowering 'Mme. Salleron' geranium (1845-50) was a favorite for Victorian bedding-out schemes.

Many other treasures are also found in neighborhood gardens, but watch out for the "trifids," or those that propagate themselves excessively and become impossible to eradicate, such as the variegated goutweed (*Aegopodium podagraria* 'Variegatum'). On the other hand, Gerard's "ladies' laces," or ribbon grass (*Phalaris arundinacea picta*) of pre-1597 is attractive in the garden and bouquets, but easily removed, as is the creeping double yellow buttercup (*Ranunculus repens* 'Pleniflorus') of pre-1629. Any garden that sports the old doubles and spurless doubles of the common columbine (*Aquilegia vulgaris* 'Flore Pleno' and 'Stellata') of pre-1572 will have them forever; the parent plants only last about three years, but their descendants become scattered all over the garden. These examples can become weeds, but what delightful weeds!

Become aware of what our ancestors grew by seeking out your neighborhood gardens. Just as an interior decorator cannot go to the corner department store and choose a coordinated room of Pennsylvania German antiques, you cannot just open up a catalog and select a complete cottage garden that reflects *you* and your specific gardening conditions. Besides, you may also make some new friends in the role of a plant preservationist. 🌿

First-year Cottage Garden

Ray Rogers

My tiny cottage garden grew out of a longstanding wish to create a green space where I lived. After residing in gardenless apartments for several years, an opportunity to move into the first floor of a house in New Brunswick, New Jersey arose. One of the house's major assets was the roughly 18 foot by 50 foot gardenable patch in the back. I jumped at the chance to fulfill my wish and, even before moving in that fall, I was busy building my own garden.

The author photographed in his New Brunswick, New Jersey first-year garden inspecting a pot of Rosmarinus officinalis *'Prostratus.'*

The garden walk photographed in late September. Among the plants photographed are: blue Aster 'Monch', red Sedum 'Autumn Joy', gray Artemisia 'Powis Castle'.

I began by inventorying the site conditions and improving undesirable ones whenever possible. Light ranged from full sun near the house to no direct sun in the rear; neighboring buildings provided wind protection for most of the site; and the soil worked easily and held moisture well. A newly laid asphalt parking area along the north and east, a picket fence and lawn to the west and a garage and three-story house along the south and southeast bordered the area. Piles of pebbles and mulch lay all over. As I dug around, I unearthed plastic sheets and several well-decayed boards—remnants of a long-gone vegetable garden.

Ray Rogers lives in New Brunswick, New Jersey, and works at Atlock Flower Farm, a perennial/topiary/everlastings nursery in nearby Somerset. He has gardened all his life, and worked at the Morris Arboretum of the University of Pennsylvania, the American Horticultural Society and Colonial Park in Somerset.

The plastic and the boards came out easily, and I raked most of the pebbles and mulch along the asphalt and garage foundation. Climatic conditions and the asphalt presented greater challenges. My biggest concern was coping with the radiating heat along the asphalt. I knew I wanted to grow interesting things in that area, so I listed heat- and drought-tolerant plants that would survive and, better still, thrive in soil loaded with pebbles: sedums, sempervivums, portulaca, miniature irises, junipers, lavender cotton (*Santolina chamaecyparissus*) and others.

I figured the other climate and soil conditions would reveal their suitability as the plants went through the seasons, so I felt I didn't need to spend a lot of time matching plants to the rest of the site. I did want to grow some things I knew would need shade, so those ended up in the rear of the garden or in the shadow of larger plants and the fence. One of the happiest associations was the variegated grouping of polka dot plant (*Hypoestes*

21

'Pink Splash'), striped lilyturf (*Liriope* 'Silver Dragon'), and lungwort (*Pulmonaria saccharata* 'Mrs. Moon'). All thrived in the shade of a venerable tree peony, which grew in nearly full sun.

Before designing or installing anything, however, the next step was to evaluate the existing plants. The tree peony was among the few plants which survived the resulting purge. I removed all but one each of the many roses and volunteer phlox, and I eventually eradicated the grasses and thistles. A yew, four herbaceous peonies, a clump of unknown iris, and seedling larkspur and sweet william catchfly (*Silene armeria*) completed the survivors' list. By then the site was cleaned up and ready for on-site planning.

After measuring the basic garden dimensions and drawing a fairly accurate diagram on graph paper, I went to the second floor windows to visualize the locations of the patio, walk, specimen plants and general planting areas. After many mental rearrangements I marked the rough layout with bonemeal. I hoped I hadn't allowed too much space for the patio and walk, thinking about the hundreds of plants I wanted to squeeze into less than 700 square feet. But a voice kept telling me I would want a sizeable patio and walk to accommodate garden visitors as the sweet alyssum and other creepers spread over the bluestone.

Because of time and budget constraints, I did not lay the patio and walk until the following summer. Happily, that presented few problems since I had anticipated the locations of those features as I planted. Only a few plants had to be moved as I juggled the stones into place. However, if I have more time when creating a similar garden, I'll be sure to lay the basic structures before doing any adjacent planting.

From the beginning, three documents guided me as I planned the garden: a plant list, a bulb location map and a journal.

The plant list recorded over 200 plants that first year, and the bulb map prevented unfortunate unearthings during spring and summer as I added, transplanted or removed those 200 plants. The journal included bloom times, ideas for combinations, successes and failures and a bundle of useful information. Taken together, they became an indispensable tool for planning, managing and enjoying my very personal garden.

Five general principles guided me through the first year:

1. Pay close attention to sound horticultural practices.

2. Grow only plants suited to the conditions and "look" of the garden.

3. Plan and plant according to fundamental design principles of color, repetition and scale.

4. Emphasize a good foliage framework, and extend the season with plants of early and late interest.

5. Experiment, expect change and work with the plants.

The soil test, done before anything went into the ground, indicated very slightly alkaline soil high in potassium and phosphorus. Occasional applications of liquid acid fertilizer helped poky and yellowing plants, and virtually everything received a dose of liquified seaweed at planting time. I believe my conservative approach with fertilizer prevented excessively lush growth and fostered good bloom.

A two-inch layer of pine needles, plus the existing bark chips and pebbles, provided an excellent mulch. As the plants grew and filled in, they became their own mulch, conserving moisture and smothering virtually all of the weeds. Although planting at close quarters created a few problems, it basically paid off in quick soil cover and an almost immediate knit-together look.

Choosing the select few for my tiny garden was perhaps the best and the worst part of the entire creative process. Certain plants were indispensable, including *Artemisia* 'Powis Castle', *Sedum* 'Autumn Joy', and *Juniperus squamata* 'Blue Star'. However, I knew that no matter how well they might grow in other gardens, if they grew poorly in my garden, they would be removed. Why waste effort on inferior plants?

Visitors were often surprised at the variety of plants growing happily together. I decided from the beginning that I wouldn't limit myself exclusively to annuals or perennials or to some other narrow list. With my "only the best" principle as a guide, I enjoyed annuals, perennials, biennials, deciduous and evergreen shrubs, bulbs, herbs, vines and, to my constant pleasure, fragrant flowers and foliage.

It would be futile to grow superior plants with no thought given to sound design principles. Playing with color, like choosing the plants, became a love/hate affair. I wanted to adhere to a basic color scheme, but I would kick myself for excluding plants of "unacceptable" colors. As it turned out, my cool scheme of blue, purple, dark red, magenta, pink, green, gray, white and black accommodated plenty of very satisfactory plants, including a few pale-yellow-flowered *Coreopsis* 'Moonbeam'. They created a beautiful picture, quite cooling on hot days.

Oenothera drummondii

Because of space limitations, I could not repeat the same plants for the sake of unity. Instead, I repeated similar forms and colors. The most pleasing were the gray mounds of *Santolina*, sage, curry plant (*Helichrysum angustifolium*), and lavender providing a foil for bright magenta and red-violet blooms of *Liatris* 'Kobold', *Lythrum* 'Happy', and purple coneflower (*Echinacea purpurea*) 'Magnus', among others.

The judicious use of a few large plants prevented the garden from looking like a collection of 200 dwarfs. So did the patio and walk, whose large mass tied everything together and blended nicely with the many colors and forms.

I paid particular attention to good foliage and to plants with early and late season interest. Besides the evergreens, many herbaceous plants provided important company for the cameo roles of flowers, including *Fritillaria persica's* dramatic spirals and the threadlike veils of dill and fennel. Crocuses and inch-tall *Sedum acre* provided color in early March; late-flowering lavender *Aster tataricus*, blooming on seven-foot stems, and the diminutive *Sedum sieboldii* with pink flowers and blue leaves stretched the season into November.

Even though my primary goal was to create a finished-looking garden within a year, I planned for further seasons. Resisting the urge to deadhead some annuals insured seeds for next year's plants, and many of the perennials would increase in width and general strength. Some plants would die; others would do too well and would have to be thinned. Unpredictability and constant change in a dynamic garden produce challenges and successes; failures can be recorded and remembered.

During my garden's first year, I enjoyed a parade of hundreds of plants, their qualities and quirks. In one year the weedy patch I adopted had become, with a little planning and effort, a dream realized.

The Top 20 Plants After One Year

Four basic criteria guided me in the selection of these as the cream of the crop: sturdy growth habit, attractive flowers, interesting foliage and pleasing fragrance.

Annuals

Foeniculum vulgare (green fennel). Quickly grows to four feet with yellow umbrella flowers and threadlike anise-scented leaves. Reseeds.

Lobularia maritima cultivars (sweet alyssum). Low, spreading mounds of white ('Snow Crystals') or purple ('Royal Carpet') honey-scented flowers. Easy and long-flowering, and reseeds.

Monarda citriodora (annual bergamot). Impressive three-foot purple spikes and fragrance of Earl Grey tea. Variable growth habit; save seeds of superior forms for next year.

Nicotiana alata 'Grandiflora' (white flowering tobacco). Open clusters of starry white trumpets emit a haunting fragrance

Top: The walk as seen across the page in July. Yellow Coreopsis *'Moonbeam'; purple alyssum 'Royal Carpet' on either side. The large head is* Cleome *with* Verbena bonariensis *silhouetted against the gray garage.*

on warm evenings. Grows to three feet and responds well to deadheading. Reseeds.

Pelargonium cultivars (scented geraniums). Both slow-growing 'Mabel Gray' (mindful of lemon furniture polish) and spreading 'Gray Lady Plymouth' (rose) dry well for potpourri. Handsome foliage; usually grow under two feet.

Perennials

Alchemilla vulgaris (lady's-mantle). Greenish-yellow flowers seem to last forever above pleated soft green leaves. New foliage in late summer freshens the clump. Never exceeds one foot.

Coreopsis 'Moonbeam'. Spreading slowly but surely, these one-foot mounds of dark green leaves bear pale yellow stars for

Photos by Harry Haskell

Top: *Just a few weeks before the photograph opposite the garden displays* Phlox *'Dodo Hanbury Forbes', white* Nicotiana, *yellow* Coreopsis *'Moonbeam'. In the foreground are tuberose, lavender, scented geranium 'Gray Lady Plymouth'.*

Bottom: *A late September photograph shows silver* Artemisia *'Powis Castle', red* Sedum *'Autumn Joy', and blue* Ruta officinalis *'Blue Curl'.*

months. Easy, adaptable to some shade and peerless.

Sedum 'Autumn Joy'. Compact mounds of thick leaves support large flower clusters which turn from green to pink to reddish to rust. Irresistible to insects, especially butterflies and honeybees. Grow in lean soil in sun; reaches two feet.

Sedum 'Vera Jameson'. Six-inch open mounds of green/purple/blue leaves and pink flowers open slowly from pinkish buds. Reliable and tough in full sun.

Sedum sieboldii (October daphne; not to be confused with the shrubby genus *Daphne*). Rounded blue scalloped leaves all summer with purplish edges. Pink flowers add color to late-season display. Rarely as tall as six inches, tolerates quite a bit of shade but at the expense of flowers.

Biennials

Dianthus superbus 'Longicalycinus'. Never very robust-looking, it nevertheless produces sizable clusters of pink clove-and-sugar scented fringed flowers for months. About one foot and easy from fresh seed.

Subshrubs

Artemisia 'Powis Castle'. Surprisingly hardy and vigorous, this is the ultimate silver-gray contrast for pink, purple, magenta and blue flowers and leaves. Pungent lacy foliage spreads widely and may reach 30 inches tall. Protect where questionably hardy and cut back drastically in spring—to eight inches or even less—to keep compact.

Chrysanthemum nipponicum (Nippon daisy). Essentially a shrubby, fall-blooming Shasta daisy up to 30 inches. Shiny dark green leaves show white flowers to perfection in October. Hardy; prune to six inches or so in spring.

Helichrysum angustifolium (curry plant; inedible). Dead ringer for scent of commercial curry powder. Fine-textured gray leafy mounds to two feet; pull off yellow flower buds for compact plant. Grow in well-drained soil and cover thickly in severe winters.

Juniperus squamata 'Blue Star'. Slow growing, low (to one foot after several years), bright gray-blue foil for pink-flowered neighbors. Needs full sun and good drainage for best growth. Very hardy.

Ruta graveolens (rue). Common rue is a grayish green, sharply scented shrublet to two feet. 'Blue Curl' is shorter, slower, quite blue and may be slow to establish. Cut back hard in spring for compact form and fewer flowers.

Rosmarinus officinalis 'Prostratus' (prostrate or weeping rosemary). Ideal for containers; water heavily in hot weather. Pine-scented needlelike leaves are useful for cooking. Profuse light blue flowers appear if grown in full sun. Bring into cool sunny spot for winter and reduce water. Variable height and twisted growth.

Salvia officinalis (sage). Faintly musty scent makes a welcome contrast to sweet and spicy fragrances. Grow in lean, well-drained soil in full sun; cut back in spring. Tends to flop as it tries to reach two feet. Protect lightly in winter.

Santolina chamaecyparissus (lavender cotton). Silver-gray tiny leaves on 12-inch buns. Sun and lean soil encourage tight growth; cut back hard in spring. Odd musky scent.

Santolina virens (green santolina). Larger, green version of the above. Same scent and culture. Both may flop open in spite of your best efforts; the green fills in faster than the silver to produce a low green pancake.✿➤

Ocimum (basil)

Pass-along

Gardens

Felder Rushing

Pass-alongs. They're there, in every community, every rural route and neighborhood, quietly being slipped from hand to hand, garden to garden. Each has a unique value begging to be shared among gardeners, giving it a special place in the world of cultivated plants. True, many of these heirlooms are "old fashioned," and possess unique beauty, fragrance, hardiness, tolerance of many sites and soils, herbal uses or other strong points. Yet what makes plants "pass-alongs" is the ease and regularity with which they can be propagated and given away. It is said that such plants afford our only opportunity to divide and multiply at the same time.

Some have been preserved and cherished for many generations. Others may be new to the horticultural scene, or recently revived in either original or improved form and therefore new to an area. Still others are so easily grown—or so invasive—that their best uses are for encouraging new gardeners in a sort of "confidence building" scheme.

Since it's impossible to give or receive

plants without at least a word of cultural advice, each one comes with an experience, a tip, often a story. Bonds are developed between those gardeners who share their plants, and special feelings grow between each gardener and his landscape. In turn, these attitudes invite more sharing.

By the way, there's a superstitious Southern tradition, surprisingly common, which holds that if you thank someone for a plant it won't grow. Upon hearing this from a grateful recipient, it follows that the proper response is to simply say, "That's right, honey," and let it go.

Another quality, if you'd call it that, of pass-alongs is their relative scarcity in the commercial marketplace. They are rarely found in the trendy "one stop shopping centers" which seem to be the new norm. In bygone days, a few unusual plants could be found at family-owned nurseries that grew their own stock and sold freshly-dug plants. Itinerant, seasonal peddlers brought herbs, seed and cuttings.

The past decade has seen an encouraging increase in small, specialty nurseries devoted to finding and promoting old or hardy perennials and shrubs. Mail-order firms, old and new alike, have always done a good job of making available unusual plants. Many a gardener has "gone in" with another on a mail order, intending to swap cuttings or divisions the next year.

Felder Rushing is an award-winning author, garden columnist and longtime host of a live radio program and TV program. He travels extensively in Southern gardens, gives lectures on native plants and is co-author of a book on Southern pass-along plants with fellow gardener and writer Steve Bender.

Crinum, *milk-and-wine, appears in almost every neighborhood or country garden in the South.*

Elizabeth Lawrence's *Gardening for Love* (Duke University Press, 1987) provides pass-along gardeners with a major reference on old plants and their "sweet country names," as well as a fascinating peek into garden souls and cottage gardens of the South and Southeast. Hundreds of plants are mentioned, and there are also lists of mail order sources and addresses of market bulletins through which these cherished plants may be located.

A classic pass-along plant is Dioscorea bulbifera, *commonly known as "'tater vine." The airborne tubers must be harvested before the first frost, stored over winter indoors and replanted each spring.*

Night-blooming cereus, Hylocereus, *is an exotic looking pot plant that is a common pass-along.*

One of the best places to find pass-along plants (and their gardeners) is at county or state flower shows. Put on by garden clubs, plant societies and extension homemaker clubs, these shows are ideal settings for pass-along gardeners to meet and swap.

Many of these plants are experiencing a revival and becoming central to our exciting new national gardening style, of which cottage gardening is an important part. Seminars are bringing attention to designers, gardeners and writers whose work has highlighted the variety and practicality of hardy plants, especially perennials, annuals and their woody companions. Several beautifully illustrated books are now available, including William Welch's *Perennial Garden Color* (Taylor Publishing, 1989), Madalene Hill's *Southern Herb Growing* (Shearer Publishing, 1987), Neil Odenwald's *Southern Plants*

Antique Bulbs for Cottage Gardens

Scott G. Kunst

The madonna lily, Lilium candidum, *appears in Minoan frescoes from about 1600 B. C. It was valued for its beauty, fragrance and medicinal virtues. The waxy white blossoms are striking in the June garden.*

Part of the appeal of cottage gardens is their old-fashioned charm, and most cottage gardens include old-fashioned plants. Though herbs and old roses may be most common, there are plenty of others—primroses, bleeding-heart, sweet william, forget-me-not. To add to the old-fashioned ambience of your cottage garden, consider antique bulbs. Generally colorful, easy to care for and fragrant, they have been grown and loved by generations of cottage gardeners. Though many have vanished, the almost three dozen survivors described here are still commercially available.

The so-called minor bulbs have played a major role in cottage gardens for centuries. Snowdrops (*Galanthus nivalis,* introduced into gardens by 1597) are usually the first flowers of spring. Their nodding white bells smell faintly of honey, a great treat in March. For early, pure blue, nothing can compare with Siberian squill (*Scilla sibirica*). Though a relative newcomer to gardens (it first became popular in Victorian times), squill is often found naturalized in old gardens. So is the gloriously fragrant lily-of-the-valley (*Convallaria majalis*). A shade-loving British native, it was being enjoyed in gardens by the 1500s or earlier.

Landscape historian Scott G. Kunst gardens in Ann Arbor, Michigan. He researches and consults on landscape preservation, teaches courses in American landscape history at Eastern Michigan University and writes frequently for the Old-House Journal.

Though species or "snow crocus" are increasingly popular today, the large Dutch hybrids have always been more common. 'Mammoth Yellow', for example, has been a fixture in gardens since before 1665. Its purple and white cousins entered European gardens at roughly the same time, though the oldest available cultivars are 'Purpureus Grandiflorus' (a warm purple from about 1870) and 'King of the Striped' (1880). One species crocus that was common in older gardens is *Crocus susianus* or 'Cloth of Gold' (by 1587, also known as *C. angustifolius*). In bloom it covers the ground with short, dense masses of bright gold flowers.

Tulips have been garden favorites since their introduction from Constantinople in the 1550s, and several historic cultivars can still be found. 'Keizerskroon' (1750) is a stocky plant with deep gold and wine-red blooms. 'Couleur Cardinal' (1815) is a rich red, shaded with plum. The scarlet 'Prince of Austria' (1860) is highly scented, while the rosy purple of 'Van der Neer' (1860) makes it a favorite of mine.

Top: *Tiger lilies were the first Oriental lilies to reach the West. It is a true lily with sturdy three- to five-foot stalks that carry dozens of pendulous, turk's cap flowers.*

Bottom: *Once exceedingly popular, the graceful Campernelle daffodil, N. x odorus, is bright yellow, short cupped and fragrant.*

Unfortunately, none of the old "broken" or streaked tulips—once the most prized—are commercially available today. To substitute, try the modern 'Cordell Hull', 'Sorbet' or the so-called Rembrandts.

Perhaps closest to the original Turkish garden tulips is the pale yellow and red *Tulipa marjolettii*. Though still classified as a species, it is apparently a very old garden variety that escaped and naturalized in Italy where it was rediscovered—along with other "neo-tulips"—in the 1800s.

Other true species tulips have long been grown by discriminating gardeners. The dainty, red-and-white striped *T. clusiana* (by 1636), for example, and the nodding, yellow *T. sylvestris* (formerly *T. florentina*, by 1629) were both grown by Thomas Jefferson at Monticello.

Though sometimes considered stiff and formal, hyacinths deserve a place in the cottage garden because of their long history (which parallels that of the tulip) and powerful fragrance. Several cultivars common today date back to the hyacinth's Victorian heyday, including 'L'Innocence' (white, 1863), 'Lady Derby' (pink, 1875), and 'City of Haarlem' (pale yellow, 1893). Looking more antique with their small spikes and unusual colors are 'Distinction', a deep maroon from 1880, and 'Oranje Boven', a salmon-pink from 1870. Two old double hyacinths are the lavender 'General Kohler' (about 1878) and 'Chestnut Flower' (1880) with narrow, loosely set spikes of starry pink florets. All are fragrant.

Another Turkish contribution to our cottage gardens is the exotic-looking crown imperial (*Fritillaria imperialis*, 1576). In spring its three-foot stalks are topped by a crown of red, orange, or yellow bells with a tuft of green leaves above them. Though some gardeners are put off by its smell—reminiscent of a skunk—for others this only adds to its freakish charm. To keep crown imperial from disappearing, try planting it on its side in a bucketful of pure sand in a spot that never gets too wet or icy.

Though daffodils came into their golden age in the early 20th century, several varieties had been well-loved for centuries before that. *Narcissus* x *medioluteus* (formerly *N.* x *biflorus,* by 1629) is common in old gardens in the mid-Atlantic and southern states. Known by many names—'Primrose Peerless', 'Twin Sisters', 'Cemetery Ladies'—it flowers late in the season with two fragrant, white-petaled, yellow-cupped blooms per stem.

Another late, fragrant, historic daffodil is the 'Old Pheasant's Eye' (early 1800s, *N. poeticus recurvus*) with clean white petals and a small red-rimmed cup. Much hardier than 'Primrose Peerless', it is also found in a beautiful double form well described as gardenia flowered.

Once exceedingly popular, the graceful old 'Campernelle' daffodil (by 1601, *N.* x *odorus*) is bright yellow, short cupped and fragrant. Though perhaps best in USDA Zone 6 or warmer areas, it blooms in my Zone 5 garden. Its starlike double form, unfortunately, does not.

For trumpet daffodils, try the British lent lily (by 1581, *N. pseudonarcissus*). There are many subspecies, some of which look like a down-sized version of the classic 'King Alfred'. Similar in form is 'W. P. Milner' (1884), a miniature daffodil with creamy white petals and delicate yellow trumpet.

For summer bloom in the cottage garden, consider lilies, some of which are among the oldest of garden flowers. The madonna lily, *Lilium candidum*, appears in Minoan frescoes from about 1600 B.C. Valued by Roman and medieval gardeners for its beauty, fragrance and medicinal virtues, it was grown by the Pilgrims in their first New World gardens. Madonna lily's waxy white blossoms are striking in the June garden, but even better is its intoxicating fragrance.

Tiger lilies were the first Oriental lilies to reach the West, arriving in 1804. Not to be confused with the orange daylily, *Lilium tigrinum* is a true lily with sturdy three- to five-foot stalks that carry dozens of pendulous, turk's-cap flowers of a strong, odd orange. In old gardens, tiger lily often blooms alongside magenta phlox, artlessly clashing in true cottage-garden fashion. Though reputedly prone to virus infection (as is the madonna lily), in most gardens the tiger lily grows vigorously.

The list of antique bulbs goes on and on: martagon and other lilies, naked ladies (*Lycoris*), tuberose, other daffodils, an array of grape hyacinths, nodding star-of-Bethlehem and so on. In the flowery profusion of your cottage garden, may you always find room for one more. ❀

The Cottage Gardens
of Texas

Dr. William C. Welch

The typical Texas cottage garden was a small front dooryard, enclosed by fence or hedge. A walk—usually packed dirt, brick or stone—led to the front steps. In this small area, the gardener planted every sort of flowering greenery. The object was to have as great a display of bloom as the season allowed. This garden was hoed to keep down weeds during the growing season, and "inspired" by shovelsful of cow barn and chicken coop manure in the winter. The backyard was often separately enclosed, and in common with most of the lower South, was "swept" with a "besom" (a broom of twigs), usually by a child of the family. Often this was done because chickens were allowed to forage in the back yard. This gardening tradition was followed largely by rural working class folk, both white and black. Mexican-Texans were also renowned for their flowering dooryards, and their aim was also to produce the most colorful display possible. Northern European immigrants to Texas, especially the German influx of the 1840s and '50s, also had dooryard gardening traditions.

The cottage garden in Texas had its beginnings in the Spanish *presidios* of the 17th and 18th centuries, though no records describe them. A later visitor to San Antonio did document the *labores* or small farms that lined the San Antonio River in 1843, recalling the flowers, orchards and vegetables intermixed in these plots. The Church, here as in Europe during the Dark Ages, preserved and introduced plants, especially flowers, to decorate the altars during church festivals.

Mrs. Mary Austin Holley, cousin of Texas' first Anglo colonizer Stephen F. Austin, wrote an immigrant guide to the new Mexican state (1821-1836). In her diary, she sketched some of the early homes built in the coastal section. The house of her brother, Henry Austin, near Brazoria on the Brazos River was one subject of her pencil in 1835. She showed the huge 'Old Blush' rose bushes lining the walk and the multiflora roses running over "a good fence . . . to form a hedge." She also mentioned the 'Old Blush' planted in the family burial plot with figs placed outside the fence.

Dr. William C. Welch is Extension Landscape Horticulturist for the Texas A & M University system and lives in College Station, Texas. He currently serves as Landscape Design Chairman for the National Council of State Garden Clubs and recently completed a book on perennials and old garden roses entitled Perennial Garden Color, *published by Taylor Publishing Company, Dallas, Texas.*

35

Emily West de Zavala, second wife of the Texas patriot, planted her garden at Lynchburg (near present Houston) as events sparked the Texas Revolution. Her granddaughter recalled how this garden was arranged and what plants it included, for in later years, when the widowed Emily remarried and moved to Galveston, she moved her plants and arranged them in the same way. Her Classical Revival East Texas house had the climbing form of the rose 'Cramoisi Superieur' on the west corner of the porch and the yellow 'Lady Banksia' on the east. A large magnolia anchored the west front corner of the picket-fenced dooryard, and an old cape jasmine graced the east corner. In between was a graduated border with the beds lined in violas, pansies, forget-me-nots and johnny-jump-ups. The middle of these beds had pinks, verbenas, geraniums, larkspur, pink Texas Stars and lady's slipper. (Some of these were native to the area and probably collected nearby.) Moss and tea roses were planted along the fence. Irises

Top: *This south central garden contains Texas bluebonnets, annual phlox, old garden roses and herbs.*

Bottom right: Gladiolus byzantinus *was found in an east Texas cemetery where it had grown undisturbed for many years increasing over that period of time.*

This re-creation of a turn of the century Texas garden contains old roses, perennials and annuals. There are very few authentic cottage gardens still extant in rural Texas, but plants may be found in old cemeteries and house sites.

37

were planted in the west side yard followed by herbs mixed with cockscomb, bachelor-buttons, "old maids" (unimproved kinds of zinnias), hollyhocks, marigolds and touch-me-nots. A trellis shading a garden seat was covered in roses. A specimen sour orange tree grew in the back yard, and cabbage roses lined the rear walk. A lone double-flowered pink althea stood guard by the front gate.

Of the plants in this early Texas garden, the annuals probably were purchased originally as seed, and then would have reseeded yearly. The forms of zinnias, cockscombs and marigolds would not have been the impressive sorts currently available—the product of quite recent 20th century hybridizers — but rather some near-species types. Some of the roses were received as parting gifts when de Zavala retired as Mexico's minister to France in 1835. These were evidently the latest products of the French breeders and as yet unknown in the New World. In her Galveston garden, Emily later grew a fine collection of roses including 'Marechal Niel', 'Catherine Mermet', 'Ducher', 'Paul Neyron', 'La France' and 'Salet'.

German immigration had a tremendous impact on Texas during the 1840s and 50s. One 1845 observer wrote that the gardens of the "older cities"— such as Galveston, Houston, and San Antonio—contained chinaberry trees (*Melia azedarach*), oleanders, crape-myrtles, altheas, retama trees (*Parkinsonia aculeata*), Texas mountain laurel (*Sophora secundiflora*), catalpas, locust trees, climbing 'Cherokee' roses and many other trees and shrubs "grown in Central Europe only in hothouses."

Of these flowering shrubs the crape-myrtle had been imported from India to Europe by 1750 and had reached America by the early 19th century. The chinaberry had been grown by Thomas Jefferson at Monticello in 1776, coming from its native Asia via England in 1656. The althea was

also a Tudor introduction grown at Monticello. The 'Cherokee' rose (*Rosa laevigata*), though often considered a native, was probably imported from China into the Southern colonies, where it naturalized. Oleanders had only made their advent at Galveston a few years before, brought by a ship captain from the Caribbean to his gardening sister. Because it rooted so readily from cuttings, oleanders were already plentiful in the city by 1845.

After the Texas Republic period (1836-1846) and with the security of statehood (attained in 1846), the settlers gradually were able to concentrate on the comforts of life. They ordered seed and plants from New Orleans and the Northern states. Most local general merchandise stores in the larger towns carried flower and garden seeds by David Landreth and Co. of Philadelphia, Grant Thorburn of New York or other early companies. By the mid 1850s, nurseries were founded in New Braunfels, Victoria, Benham and Austin.

Other plant "heirlooms" were brought by settlers from their homes in other states and countries. These were often treasured reminders of home and an easier life in more settled areas. As today, neighbors and friends shared favorite plants and so increased their numbers.

Even from the earliest times, educated Texans realized the land was a treasure trove of glorious wildflowers. Emily de Zavala transplanted or seeded these into her Lynchburg garden, and perhaps others did as well.

German-born Dr. Ferdinand Jakob Lindheimer came to Texas in 1836 and was later a botanical collector. Dr. Asa Gray at Harvard and Dr. George Engelmann at St. Louis, both botanists, were two of Lindheimer's clients. He collected on the Texas Coast and in the Hill Country, and wrote to popularize the best of his finds. In 1848, he told a friend that ". . . the flora of this country offers so much that is beautiful and that the transplanting of these indigenes into gardens and flower pots is becoming more general and promises to become fashionable." Some among those he recommended were *Passiflora, Asclepias,* dark double violet clematis, *Echinacea, Lisianthus, Mirabilis,* lupines, asters and *Eryngium.*

There are very few "authentic" cottage gardens still extant in the rural areas of Texas, but occasionally old house sites, cemeteries and old towns will have plants surviving from these sorts of plantings. Spring-flowering bulbs in particular are often seen. Texas has very specific bulbs which will survive and colonize here; the most obvious are the tazetta narcissus (often called "jonquils" or "paperwhites"), *Lycoris,* hardy gladiolus, *Amaryllis, Crinum* and grape hyacinths. These mark old beds in long forgotten dooryards and their heavy fragrances recall earlier springs.

Modern collectors have found and made available through commercial sources many of the old roses. The towns of Weimar, Brenham, Navasota, Anderson, the older residential sections of Bryan, Paige, Bastrop, San Marcos, East Columbia, Frelsburg, San Antonio, Shelby, Castroville, New Braunfels and Victoria are noted for their old shrub roses. Many teas and chinas and some early polyanthas, noisettes, bourbons, ramblers and gallicas are the classes that generally survive summer heat in this area. One lovely cream-colored tea has been found in Laredo on the Rio Grande—a tribute to its summer hardiness!

Of other perennials, several irises survive here. The most common is *Iris x albicans,* the old white flag, which is often planted in cemeteries. A lavender form also exists. Louisiana irises may be found on the coast and in East Texas. Native hibiscus, known as "marshmallows," are abundant in low areas of East Texas. All mallows act as perennials in the southern half of the state and were often planted. Wild violets and wild ageratum favor damp places and were often used in gardens. Wormwood (*Artemisia*), bouncing bet (*Saponaria*) and yarrow (*Achillea*) were also perennial favorites.

Mexican petunia (*Ruellia*) is native to Mexico and has naturalized in much of Texas. Petunialike blue-purple flowers appear on tall stems from spring through fall, even in the hottest, driest weather. *Justicia* is often seen in San Antonio along with the bird-of-paradise shrub (*Caesalpinia gilliesii*), castor beans, Barbados cherry (*Malpighia glabra* x *M. punicifolia*), spineless forms of Opuntia and ghost plant (*Graptopetalum paraguayense*).

Small trees often found in cottage gardens include pomegranate, native plums, figs, mulberries (for the chickens), persimmon and chinaberry. Large trees were generally avoided as they gave too much shade for the flowers.

Vines were used to shade the porches and patios of Texans and many were multi-purpose kinds. Queen's crown, all sorts of grapes, cypress vine (*Ipomoea quamoclit*), scarlet runner beans, morning-glories, balloon vine (*Cardiospermum halicacabum*) and passionflower are among the most commonly mentioned. Madeira vine (*Anredera cordifolia*), a fragrant, tender climber with greenish-white panicles, was much used in Victorian days as well.

These surviving plants and sparse writings of early travelers and immigrants are the meager sources of information on old Texas cottage gardens. Newspaper ads and nursery catalogs of the period also provide clues about what was grown. This information is important not only for historical interest, but also because the present need to conserve water in Texas makes the summer-tough yet generously flowering plants used in old cottage gardens very precious. In their cottage gardens our ancestors completed a very comprehensive plant testing program—one that lasted 150 years! ❦

A Cottage Garden
New Mexico Style

Ellen Reed

A New Englander transplanted to a semidesert, I chose this home 21 years ago because of its lush backyard set off from its neighbors by high evergreen shrubs and shaded by 20-year-old trees. The front yard was a steeply sloping bluegrass and bermuda grass lawn

with large evergreen foundation plantings, a weeping willow astride the sewer line, a four-headed blue spruce and a mildew-prone lilac. The backyard also included sun-starved floribunda and hybrid tea roses, eight huge arborvitaes, several large junipers, photinias, *Euonymus japonica*, a

Ellen Reed grew up in Maine, where she learned gardening from her grandmother. Since then she has lived and gardened in Germany, Japan and—for the last 20 years—in Albuquerque, New Mexico.

In the back garden the fence provides a backdrop for summerblooming impatiens and Catharanthus roseus.

The front garden slopes steeply down to the street. In spring narcissus, 'Red Jade' crabapple and Spirea thunbergii *provide the accents in this area.*

honey locust, two mountain cottonwoods and a lovely 'Kwanzan' cherry.

The 100 foot by 170 foot lot is divided by a long, low, white house into a 40-foot deep steeply sloping, eastern-facing front yard and a 60-foot deep flat backyard with a small hourglass-shaped pond and waterfall to the south. There is a curved, cement, 30 foot by 15 foot patio along the back of the house. The honey locust was in a mid-lawn island.

We are in an established neighborhood in Albuquerque, New Mexico. Average annual precipitation of seven to ten inches occurs mostly in July with some rapidly melting snow between November and April. There is a 20 to 30 degree daily temperature fluctuation, so the ground usually thaws during sunny winter days. Our 100-degree days may occur for a week in June and lows in the teens come in January or February. May 15 to October 15

are our frost-free dates and high winds are expected in April. We are classified as high desert, USDA Zone 6. Humidity generally is 10 to 30 percent. In order to grow other than dryland plants, it is necessary to irrigate once or twice a month in winter and two or three times a week during the growing season.

Bluegrass and bermuda grass lawns and evergreen foundation plantings are the norm in established neighborhoods, with Southwest landscapes of juniper, pinyon pine and yucca in a sea of gravel prevailing in newer developments. Purple-leaf plum and 'Hopa' crabs are the most common ornamental trees with orange pyracantha, pampas grass, Spanish broom and various cotoneasters frequent accents. *Ulmus pumila* (Siberian elm) and honey locust are common shade trees in older areas and fruitless mulberries or London plane trees in newer ones.

41

The most memorable part of my garden used to be the secluded backyard but is now the inviting front garden with its winding welcoming path leading through ever-changing colors and forms. This is due in part to natural catastrophes, to happenstance and to some recent planning. The blue spruce blew over, a cottonwood died of borers and large photinias and euonymus shrubs froze in a record -17 F degrees in 1971. The weeping willow was removed when Roto-Rooter had to come for the second time. I missed it for about a week until I realized its sunny spot could be filled with flowering shrubs and perennials. The lawns retreated by a shovel's width per year as I collected more interesting plants. Even with my limited design training I realized the chaos which could develop from my passion for one of everything. The white house with its red door set my original patriotic color scheme, which has broadened to include all but the flaming purples and magentas. I have added trees and shrubs with mostly red or white flowers. Pesky plants have been eliminated and replaced by ones with several seasons' beauty or off-season interest.

After exhausting local nurseries I succumbed to the lure of the photographs and descriptions in mail-order catalogs. I discovered the reliable ones and how to check flamboyant prose with a garden encyclopedia. If it says "needs constant moisture" or "hates lime," it's not for Albuquerque. Also, many dryland natives will not tolerate supplemental watering or less than full sun. However, my semi-shade is enough for many Eastern sun lovers. The eastern slope of my front garden protects heaths (*Erica* cultivars) from the burning afternoon sun and provides the rapid drainage preferred by many bulbs and perennials.

A microclimate under an arching juniper by the front entrance allows me to grow three low azaleas, *Bletilla striata* (Chinese ground orchid) and *Athyrium goeringianum* 'Pictum' (Japanese painted fern). There, also, the spotted leaves of *Zantedeschia albomaculata* (hardy calla lily) are replaced in the fall by the white-veined arrowheads (*Arum italicum*). *Mimulus* hybrids have become established along with volunteer 'Cambridge Blue' lobelias at the juniper drip line.

My love affair with bulbs began when I was a child and read *The Secret Garden* by Frances Hodgson Burnett. Many of the minor bulbs became too prolific and had to be eliminated from the central raised rockery which I designed to camouflage the honey-locust stump. *Tulipa clusiana* and *T. chrysantha* are still established here and their invasive foliage smothers less hardy neighbors such as dwarf narcissi. Other less aggressive species tulips enjoy the drainage provided by additional volcanic scoria and pumice in the rockery. Several saxifrages, hebes, penstemons, sedums and *Androsace* (rock jasmine) have spread their roots in the cooler areas under the rocky ledge. On the east end of this raised area several dwarf heaths (*Erica* spp.), *Papaver burseri* (alpine poppy), *Geranium sessiliflorum* 'Nigrum' and *Chrysanthemum ptarmiciflorum* have woven themselves together very satisfactorily. Numerous snowdrops (*Galanthus* spp.), species crocus, hybrid cyclamens and dwarf narcissus add early interest. *Anemone sylvestris* is proving too well adapted here and will have to be restrained. A large *Ilex aquifolium* 'San Gabriel' has developed well since the locust tree's removal and provides height to this central bed. Under the holly, leaves of *Cyclamen hederifolium* provide a beautiful winter ground cover after its dainty flowers are past. Bordering this island at lawn level are *Campanula elatines garganica*, *Ajuga reptans* 'Burgundy Lace', *Viola cornuta* 'Blue Perfection' and *Geranium dalmaticum*.

The design of the garden became more pronounced after the children (my lawn mowers) left home and I smoothed out some of the sharpest curves of the back flower beds and eliminated the nooks of lawn by setting stepping stones in a mix of creeping veronicas and thymes. The steep, cracked, concrete front walk dividing the sloping lawn was replaced with a gradually ascending path bordered by granite boulders from the nearby Sandia Mountain foothills. Several groupings of steps are formed of granite and the walk surface is finely crushed gravel, which has proven a wonderful seed bed. Many seedlings are repotted for sharing, replanting or donating to the Albuquerque Garden Center plant sale.

The front is accented on the northwest with a 'Red Jade' crabapple balanced on the southeast by a group of white-flowered shrubs: *Spiraea thunbergii, S. prunifolia, Abeliophyllum distichum,* a large treelike cotoneaster (*C. hupehensis*), *Vitex agnus-castus* 'Alba', *Buddleia davidii* 'White Profusion' and a double white lilac. Several weigelas recently added are much appreciated by the hummingbirds.

After unsuccessful attempts to disguise the peeling paint of the back cinderblock wall with ivy and evergreen shrubs, I removed all the ivy, which preferred to creep into the garden anyway, and had a six-foot cedar stake fence constructed as a neutral background on the west and north sides. Now I am surrounded by my neighbors' treetops.

Spring flower display begins with snowdrops, *Hamamelis* x *intermedia* 'Arnold Promise' (witch hazel), *Adonis amurensis, Eranthis* (winter aconite), *Erythronium* cultivars (glacier lilies), species crocus, *Erica* cultivars (heaths), *Helleborus lividus, H. foetidus* and *H. orientalis* (lenten rose) and *Anemone pulsatilla* (pasque-flower). Early and late narcissi and hyacinths continue the show. Botanical tulip cultivars (*T. greigii, T. kaufmanniana, T. fosteriana*), Darwin hybrids and lily-flowered tulips, which were originally planted in groups of

five to 12, have persisted and increased when planted in a cold area on a one-inch layer of perlite and fertilized with superphosphate in fall or early spring. All bulb foliage is foliar fed with a balanced liquid fertilizer after bloom.

Bulb bloom is followed by self-sown blue larkspur, bachelor buttons and Shirley poppies. Forget-me-nots (*Myosotis sylvaticus*) form a sea of blue among the bulb foliage. Shrubs are pruned heavily after bloom to encourage vigor and control size. Early single peonies, *Paeonia tenuifolia* (fern-leaf peony) and tree peonies follow next. I prefer the bloom and summer foliage of Siberian iris to the more commonly grown tall bearded iris, which require more space and sun than I can provide. *Helianthemum* (sun rose), blue flax and *Eryngium maritimum* (sea holly) have proven dependable. *Filipendula vulgaris* (dropwort) was one of my early successes and is the only one of that genus to withstand spider-mite infestation. I find that cutting back foliage as well as spent bloom often rejuvenates perennials and may inspire reflowering.

Summer color is provided by a succession of native and exotic perennials supplemented with *Catharanthus roseus* 'Bright Eye', white and red impatiens and volunteer red and white *Portulaca* (moss rose), sweet alyssum and *Cosmos* 'Diablo'. About a dozen miniature roses bloom in a bed along the front walk.

Late summer brings on self-sown *Salvia coccinea* (seed collected in Texas), Monarch butterfly-attracting annual *Asclepias curassavica* as well as cushion chrysanthemums, *Salvia elegans* is pineapple sage, Japanese anemones, *Lycoris radiata* (spider lilies), *Sternbergia lutea, Colchicum autumnale* (autumn crocus) and fall crocus species. Several *Amelanchier* (shadblow or service berries), a staghorn sumac, *Hydrangea quercifolia, Ribes aureum* and pear and cherry foliage provide autumn color, as do scattered red leaves on hardy geraniums, *Mahonia aquifolium, Berberis gladwynensis* 'William Penn' and the spireas. I also enjoy the dry foliage or seed pods of Siberian iris, *Sedum spectabile* 'Autumn Joy', *Catananche* (cupid's dart) and hostas. Several crabapples, red pyracantha, dwarf cotoneaster, deciduous euonymus and hollies provide colorful berries until consumed by the birds.

In addition to the ornamental plants, I grow six Burpee 'Whopper' VFN tomatoes in cages in the front yard along with garlic, green beans and a couple of 'Ichiban' eggplants. Butter lettuce and 'Sugar Snap' peas followed by cucumbers grow in the back. Many ornamental and culinary herbs grow around the patio. A grafted pear, sour cherry, black currants and alpine strawberries provide fruit.

Nondiseased plant refuse is recycled in a compost system managed by my husband and the finished compost is used when planting or as topdressing.

My most recent experiment has been to inoculate the cottonwood stump with *Pleurotis ostreatus* (oyster mushroom spores). I am awaiting my first crop.

Plants with interesting flowers and attractive growth habit appeal to me most. Ones that need excessive pampering don't last long here. Rampant growers get composted with a few potted for the plant sale accompanied with warnings for the unwary. I particularly enjoy hardy miniature bulbs, hardy geraniums, Eastern woodland plants (I grow nine species and cultivars of violets), ericas and plants with interesting foliage. I continue to try new plants whether from cuttings and seeds collected on trips and from friends or mail-order sources. I seldom order more than one of a kind at first as plants can usually be multiplied if they thrive here and there is not room for three of everything anyway.

More attention to native and drought-tolerant plants would cut down on my water use but I feel vindicated whenever strangers stop their cars and enjoy my colorful cottage garden. ❧

Daffodils and pasque-flower blend together in the author's garden. After the bulbs have finished, blue larkspur, bachelor buttons, Shirley poppies and forget-me-nots cover the bulb foliage.

A Western Dryland Cottage Garden

Panayoti Kelaidis

Nothing presents greater obstacles to gardening than drought. Soils can be amended, trees can be planted or cut down. But if it doesn't rain or snow, one must resort to the hose. Gardening in arid and semiarid regions is practically synonymous with watering. In order for gardeners in dry climates to take a vacation, they must first find, then cajole, bribe or beg some indebted family member or unsuspecting neighbor into indenturing themselves to a hose.

Traditionally, cottage gardens are associated with moist, even maritime, climates and most of the plants grown in them need a regular supply of moisture at the roots. Likewise, it's well known that dry regions can be floriferous. In wet years, even deserts boast rich displays of colors. But plants do not have to originate in desert to tolerate periods of drought. There are tens of thousands of ornamental plants that come from the dry steppes of Asia, from South Africa's karroo and the Patagonian pampas, from the Mediterranean maquis and phrygana, not to mention the chaparral, sagebrush and prairies of the American West.

Cottages and their gardens exist all over the world in all sorts of unlikely climates and surroundings. Isn't it theoretically

Photos by Rob Proctor

This Breckenridge, Colorado garden is described on page 73. The garden is in front of the Bay Street Company and blooms from early April until early September.

possible to combine the right plants in the right way so that even in dry climates one can re-create the floriferousness and ambience of a traditional cottage garden? This is the question Gwen Kelaidis sought to answer in designing a 60-foot border along the northern boundary of her back yard in Denver, Colorado. She had gar-

---

Panayoti Kelaidis is curator of the Rock Alpine Garden at Denver Botanic Gardens. His special interests are the conservation and cultivation of Western native plants.

dened for many years in the rich soil and well-watered summers of Wisconsin, producing a magnificent cottage garden around the shrinking patches of grass at her previous home before moving to sunny, dry Colorado. Denver is lucky to get 15 inches of rain a year, but her new home at least did have a rich clay loam and evidence that previous owners had gardened for most of the last 60 years. Despite a few years of neglect, opium poppies, annual delphiniums and even lilies were in evidence, and old plants continue to resurface years later, like forgotten memories. The long border was dug, and the worst clumps of crabgrass and bluegrass removed before a small amount of compost was spaded in and the first perennials and annuals installed.

Gwen followed the same rather simple design methods practically all cottage gardeners employ in their work: During the growing season, day after day, week after week she would come home from nurseries or plant sales with flats of plants and she would sit in front of her border looking for rapidly vanishing open places to insert her acquisitions. Plants that didn't perform to expectation were summarily moved or removed, and at times the border seemed as restless as a Balkan line dance. She was constrained by the knowledge that new plants would soon be enduring great heat and minimal supplemental irrigation. Like most gardeners, Gwen had strong prejudices and definite notions as to the colors and textures she wanted to have in this border. Although pen never touched graph paper, a complicated, integrated and wholly satisfying garden quickly came into being. Design by trowel and spade has the advantage of immediacy.

What criteria are used for planting in this garden? Obviously the plants must endure full Colorado sun and long periods of drought. As in all cottage gardens, plants are valued for their long season of bloom, vibrant and compatible colors and their ability to associate closely with neighbors. Blues, lavenders and soft pinks are valued above all other hues—although in the omnipresent, burning Colorado sun pastels need vivid yellows, whites and hot reds to provide a foil. What plants has Gwen selected, and how have they performed?

Traditional Cottage Garden Plants

Although many traditional cottage garden plants will grow in a wet climate, they do not necessarily originate there, nor do they need constant irrigation in order to perform well. Most bulbs (aside from lilies) are adapted to long periods of summer drought, and practically all crocuses, tulips, sternbergias, irises and even narcissus will survive and even thrive in long periods of summer heat and dryness. Tulips and crocuses, in particular, perform much better in dry climates than in wet. Waterlily tulips quickly form large clumps in any sunny, dry garden, and while their flowers may not be as large in subsequent years, they will persist, produce seed and self-sow if they are allowed. The many tiny scarlet tulips sold by Dutch firms as "botanicals" are particularly satisfying in Colorado: *Tulipa linifolia* opens its brassy, scarlet stars for weeks on end in our sunny, cold Aprils. *T. wilsoniana* is usually a bit more cup-shaped, with larger bells of refulgent vermilion that gradually build into magnificent clumps. The many tiny early yellow tulips can even be weedy if allowed to go to seed: *Tulipa tarda* resembles *T. urmiensis* but with pale yellow petals alternating with the brighter colored segments. Both tolerate some shade as well. These and a number of tiny crocuses like the purple violet clones of *Crocus tomasinianus* and the endless variations on *C. chrysanthus* will combine with almost any later blooming perennial, since in a dry border they do not object to being overgrown during the entire growing season. They do best mingled with plants that can be cut to the ground in fall so that the bulbs can show up unencumbered in the early spring.

Lavender (*Lavandula angustifolia*), lavender cotton (*Santolina chamaecyparissus*), rue (*Ruta graveolens*)—indeed, most garden herbs—thrive with drought. In one long extension of her dry border that Gwen calls the "herb strip," these follow on the heels of spring bulbs to provide a wonderful, long season of bloom in early summer. The yellows of rue and santolina are a perfect foil for the blues of the lavender. This tremendously successful border culminates its season when Russian sage (*Perovskia*) and butterfly weed (*Asclepias tuberosa*) reach a peak of color in July and August. These are planted throughout the strip and the lavender filigree and yellows of their bloom echo the colors of the earlier herbs. Gwen can't recall watering this garden more than once or twice a year (if that much), although it may receive a bit of runoff from the roof. It does experience the full blast of south sun, and reflection off the south side of the house and concrete path.

Although technically a shrub, *Caryopteris* x *clandonensis* is a fine addition to dry borders. Not only does it form a mound of subtle blue for much of the late season, its twiggy shape is decorative in the winter as well.

It's intriguing that many of the bright red cottage garden plants traditionally used in European cottage gardens are actually North American wildflowers. *Penstemon barbatus* grows much better and lives much longer if it dries out occasionally, and zauschnerias do not seem to require supplemental irrigation in Colorado once they are established. A vivid yellow sport of the penstemon, developed by the North Platte experiment station as 'Schooley's Yellow' is very popular in sophisticated Denver gardens. The pineleaf penstemon (*P. pinifolius*) is

another orange-red flowered native of the American Southwest that is popular around the world. In Denver it blooms most of the summer if deadheaded, and the deep green mounds of foliage are attractive at all times of the year—a perfect edging for a dry garden. *Zauschneria californica latifolia* can grow more than three feet tall, and blooms from August to frost with an intensity of orange-red that cannot be duplicated in cooler, wetter climates. Standing cypress, *Ipomopsis rubra*, from Texas is delightful both as a filigree, basal rosette its first year (like a ball of green lace), and the second year when it towers to four or five feet and produces a vivid torch of red trumpets for much of the summer season. Be sure not to deadhead this biennial if you want the performance to be repeated.

The common larkspur of cottage gardens, *Consolida ambigua*, reveals its dryland ancestry by naturalizing wildly throughout Gwen's border. She ruthlessly hoes seedlings from late autumn when they begin to germinate right up to the time they bloom, although a number of stalks are permitted to go to seed to repeat the performance next year. Although common in many people's eyes, the brilliant cobalt blues, whites and powdery pinks of this staunch winter annual give a long season of color for very little effort. *Calendula officinalis* is just as energetic a self-sowing annual, and the large orange-yellow daisies are produced for the entire growing season. These are fine "filler" plants to grow where bulbs die back, or on the fringes of the garden to create a full, cottage look. During moist years, neither requires supplemental moisture.

When one considers how many hundreds of species of *Salvia* are found in both east and west hemispheres, north and south of the equator, it is surprising that so few appear in gardens. *Salvia* contains more promise for dry gardens than almost any other genus. The brilliant selections

Another photograph of the garden at the Bay Street Company shows the garden at its peak of June bloom. It features columbines, lupines, geraniums, shasta daisies, iceland poppies and a jungle of traditional garden plants.

Little-Known Cottage Garden Plants from Dry Climates

Gwen's favorite salvia, however, is *Salvia jurisicii*, which grows up to 24 inches tall and even broader, forming a bright lavender-blue mound of color in May and June. If it is cut back hard as flowers go over, it will repeat the performance later in the summer. This salvia is restricted to a tiny area in Yugoslavia in nature, and twists its flowers so that if you examine it carefully you will find they are inverted compared to other sages. The color blends particularly well with a long border of dahlberg daisy (*Dyssodia tenuiloba*), a superlative annual from Texas that produces masses of tiny, bright yellow flowers through the

Gwen Kelaidis has established a dry border garden at her Colorado home. It contains many herbs which thrive on drought, spring bulbs, rue, santolina and lavender. The garden is not watered on a regular basis.

Photo by Sandra Snyder

and hybrids of European meadow sage (*S. x superba*) such as 'East Friesland' and 'May Night' are among the longest blooming perennials in hot climates. Their velvety blue-purples combine well with blues, yellows and whites and will last three months with judicious deadheading. The clary (*S. sclarea*) of herb gardens looks just as good in a cottage garden, and thrives under almost any cultural or moisture regime in Colorado. A somewhat more compact phase of *Salvia sclarea* introduced from Tadzhikistan has even proven perennial here. The luminous pink-purple bracts are colorful for much of the early summer, and the basal rosettes are attractive in their own right.

Photo by author

heat of the summer. Rarely seen in gardens, both plants are perfect examples of long blooming, showy and easy flowers that thrive in hot, dry summer regions.

Teucrium orientale superficially resembles a dwarf version of Balkan sage, although it originates in Anatolia and has rather larger individual flowers that have a fascinating, curlicue shape. This is another example of the many Mediterannean plants that thrive in the cold, continental climates of Western America.

A few plants are chosen primarily for their foliage: partridge feather (*Tanacetum densum amani*), bear grass (*Nolina texana*) and Himalayan catnip (*Dracocephalum calophyllum*) are attractive enough in leaf to justify space in the border. Other plants like pine-leaf penstemon (*Penstemon pinifolius*), woolly mullein (*Verbascum bombyciferum*) and dwarf culinary sage (*Salvia officinalis* 'Nana') are as beautiful in evergreen leaf as they are in bloom. So many dry-loving plants have leathery, woolly or elegantly textured foliage that foliage texture has become an important element in this dryland garden.

Like cottage gardens everywhere, Gwen's borders achieve their effect by massing hundreds of attractive flowering plants in close proximity with one another and in such a fashion that there is always color, always interest. The greatest pleasure is observing the kaleidoscopic color changes through the seasons and the years. During protracted hot and dry years, Gwen sets a sprinkler on the garden every few weeks to soak it well. The plants in the garden would undoubtedly survive without water, but flowering would be curtailed.

Dry years are so prevalent throughout much of the western United States, however, that landscape professionals are beginning to question the wisdom of relying on water-wasteful horticulture. Ten years ago, Ken Ball of the Denver Water Board invented the concept of xeriscape, which has become something of a catchword for reducing water consumption in the landscape. Xeriscape has become a lifestyle for more and more gardeners in this region, who realize that all parts of a garden need not be treated (which is to say watered) equally. Considerable water conservation can take place simply through mulching and other sensible management techniques. Of course, the secret of successful gardening in any climate is to find as many aristocratic plants as possible that grow well under your conditions, and then combine them in delightful ways. This is how Gwen Kelaidis has created a cottage garden in dry Denver clay. ❈

Like cottage gardens everywhere, Gwen's borders achieve their effect through the massing of hundreds of attractive flowering plants closely together. The colors change through the seasons.

A Streetside Cottage Garden

Ruth Rohde Haskell

The house we bought in an urban Kansas City neighborhood in 1981 sat high above the street on a terraced corner lot. Steps led up at the very corner of the property instead of straight on, giving more design interest and adding to the quaintness of the stucco house with its steeply pitched red roof. A four-foot limestone retaining wall ran across the front and along the side of the 50- × 135-foot property. Above the wall, the ground rose sharply another four feet or so in elevation, so that the basement of the home was at street level. When we'd first seen the "For Sale" sign and stopped the car, my husband had said "But what about those steep banks?" I knew immediately. "I'll dig in rocks and make a garden out of them." Those banks presented me with the most challenging, rewarding and fun gardening I've ever done.

The 135-foot-long south bank was cut by the driveway, and the back portion ran 65 feet long. Except for the area just south of the house itself, which was already terraced with railroad ties, the banks were covered with what passed for lawn—mostly crabgrass, chickweed and henbit. The west-facing bank had some *Vinca*. Because there wasn't anything there worth saving I had free rein, and I was off on a big adventure.

I turned my attention immediately to the two front portions. The west bank, across the front, was eight feet deep by 50 feet long; the south-facing bank along the side of the front yard was 10 feet deep by 35 feet long. We roto-tilled the entire front yard, banks and all, and then raked out the clods of grass and weeds—an incredible amount of work! The level part we seeded to create a small lawn. Into the slopes we anchored over half a ton of limestone carefully selected at a local quarry. The stones were there both for looks and to serve as stepping stones and perches as I worked in my future garden. That first fall I planted over 100 daffodils and a Russian olive tree, which I placed at the top of the west bank. To prevent erosion I covered the bare earth with pine needles raked from under neighborhood trees.

The following spring planting began in earnest and didn't let up for three years as I added, moved and refined. I bought many plants, but fully half the garden was populated with plants given by gardening friends. Most came as clumps dug and carried in cardboard boxes. I was lucky to count as friends several dedicated, expert gardeners who enjoy growing perennials from seed, and some of my most prized plants came to me as seedlings. Once, to my great delight, a gardener in Illinois sent seed of fringed cottage pinks, *Dianthus plumarius*, impossible to find commercially.

By and large, planning was done by eye.

I spent hours looking out of windows at the garden, through all seasons, every year. It is one of the most effective design "tools" I know.

The south bank was my pride and joy, baptized the tapestry garden because of the many gray-leaved plants that formed a muted background to the bright flower colors I prefer. On that steep slope there was no such thing as poor drainage, and the aromatic and fragrant plants I love thrived in the sun-baked soil: upright and creeping thymes, lavender, catmint, *Santolina*, yarrow, Russian sage. On a sunny day I could sit on a rock in this mediterranean microclimate, bees buzzing all around, and imagine I was on a hillside in Greece.

I used a mixture of plant forms, paying close attention to texture and stature. To take advantage of the sloping terrain I chose a combination of creeping and mat-forming plants, and cascading plants that would spill down the bank and over the top of the wall. To give height and interest, I included subshrubs and bushy plants, and some with upright forms, which I planted in drifts to give a billowing effect. All of these groups were laced together by creeping thymes, creeping oregano, ground-hugging sedums and sweet alyssum. The tallest plants on my bank were Russian sage (*Perovskia*) and coreopsis, and these I planted no farther than halfway

up the bank. I had to be careful in positioning: Tall plants at the top would look out of proportion. Tall, stiffly vertical forms were excluded; iris foliage was the most vertical form I allowed and I found it very useful to prevent the garden from looking like an unmade bed.

Below the tapestry garden, hybrid daylilies anchored the wall in a 15-inch wide planting strip. Near the steps the daylilies gave way to perennials added piece by piece from the garden above: Shasta daisies, lamb's-ears, coreopsis and hardy geranium.

The west bank also received full sun most of the day, except for about a third of its length where it was shaded by the Russian olive tree and a neighbor's silver maple. There, daffodils and grape hyacinths bloomed in the full sun of spring, succeeded by perennials tolerant of some shade, predominantly *Heuchera* and *Geranium* cultivars. I added to the existing vinca two special types, *V. minor* 'Flore Pleno' with wine-red double flowers, and 'Miss Jekyll's White', a charming, diminutive plant. In the sunny area of the west bank I continued with these plants and added creeping phlox, sweet william, dwarf lemon lily and an old pale yellow iris gathered from a friend's garden. A single plant of the eastern columbine, *Aquilegia canadensis*, self-seeded until a cloud of red and yellow blooms filled a quarter of this garden every May and June. Coreopsis also started as a single gift plant and later sprang up all through both banks and even grew out of cracks in the wall.

The strip between the base of the west wall and the sidewalk was a generous five feet. I longed to plant the entire area—50 feet long—with lavender for the sheer, fragrant joy of it, but my husband argued that lawn would better set off the garden above, and actually would be less work and could be counted on, whereas holes were certain to appear in the lavender planting. I relented, but I still harbor secret plans for, someday, a field of lavender backed by a sun-baked wall.

Right: *Early morning fog adds an ethereal quality to the author's streetside garden.*

Bottom: *The south bank became the tapestry garden because of the many gray-leaved plants. They form a muted background for the bright colors the author prefers.*

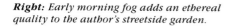

Photos by author

Above: The tapestry garden in early summer, looking east. In the foreground are Penstemon hirsutus, Achillea tomentosa *and* Nepeta mussinii; *in the middle, a single plant of* Penstemon murrayanus *with vivid orange-red flowers and coreopsis. Hybrid* Rosa wichuraiana *'May Queen' climbs the trellis.*

Below: The west bank received full sun most of the day except where the Russian olive casts its shade. In early June it perfumes the air with fragrance. Coralbells, hardy geraniums, dwarf lemon lily, Phlox subulata *and sweet william abound, and coreopsis is everywhere.*

The problems we had with these banks were weeds, most notably a healthy crop of wild onion. After a good soaking rain I would get out and with hand and trowel, pull and dig. Generally we cultivated by hand with a Cape Cod weeder, a claw-type tool and a trowel. We spent one weekend in the spring and again in the fall cleaning the banks. Thereafter most weeds could be taken care of on my morning and evening rounds when I went out to "take stock." Surprisingly, erosion was never a problem. Bare areas appeared now and then, and were either filled with plants or covered with pine needles.

Being on a corner gave our garden double exposure, and one of the greatest pleasures was the vast number of people who stopped to admire it and have a chat as we were out working. That was an aspect I hadn't counted on when I started the garden, and I enjoyed it immensely. Only once in eight years did I see someone pick a flower uninvited. 🌺

Old Roses for Today's Cottage Garden

Thomas Christopher

D rawing up a plant list for a traditional American cottage garden is a
complicated business, for in a
country as large and climatically diverse as
ours, the gardener's palette must vary from
region to region. The sweet williams of a

*Thomas Christopher studied horticulture at the
New York Botanical Garden, and is a widely
published garden writer. He is author of* In
Search Of Lost Roses, *published by Summit
Books in 1989.*

New England dooryard, for example, give
way to more heat-tolerant Drummond
phlox around a central Texas farmhouse,
while the crape-myrtles of the Deep South
are replaced by lilacs in the Midwest.
Whatever the location, though, one shrub
will always play a prominent role, and that
is the rose.

A Garden on Long Island

A Rose Garden at Thomasville, Georgia

Old-time gardeners valued this flower as much for its fragrance as its color. In the days of self-sufficiency, the rose's petals served to perfume homemade soaps and, when gathered into potpourris, to freshen the air inside the house. In addition, the rose's thorns made its canes the ideal material for an impenetrable hedge, while the gymnastic branches of a rambler could soften the appearance of the most austere masonry wall. No wonder, then, that the average cottager would as soon have left the roof off his house as the roses out of his garden.

What will strike contemporary gardeners as most remarkable, however, is that cottagers secured all these benefits with so little work. They didn't keep a weekly schedule of sprays—the only pest control they practiced was to douse each rosebush occasionally with soapy water from the dishpan. Nor did the cottagers protect their roses from winter's cold by hilling around their crowns with soil and wrapping the canes with burlap. Yet the shrubs flourished. Indeed, many plantings of a century ago still survive, blooming now beside empty cellar holes on homesteads where not only the gardener but even the house has long since passed away.

The secret of the cottagers' success was in their selection of cultivars. They planted roses of proven disease resistance, the types best adapted to the local climate and soil. These they chose by the simplest possible process. They watched their neighbors' gardens to discover the roses that grew well there, and then they borrowed a cutting. The blossoms they got in that fashion might not always win first prize at a rose show, but they were reliable, and a healthy shrub will always outshine a glamorous invalid.

When planning your cottage garden, you cannot do better than to copy the old timers. To avoid the work of rooting cuttings, you will probably wish to buy your bushes ready to plant, but even so, don't begin by opening a catalog. Instead,

'Souvenir de la Malmaisson' was named in memory of the Empress Josephine's rose garden. It is a bourbon rose and a representative of one of the oldest classes of reblooming roses.

'Old Blush' is a China rose. It forms a dense shrub as high as six feet with semi-double blush-pink flowers shaped like architectural rosettes.

Photos by Stephen Scanniello

Above: *The secret of the cottagers' success with old roses was their selection of cultivars. They watched what thrived in their neighbor's garden, then asked for a cutting. This one is 'Zephirine Droubin'.*

make an expedition around your neighborhood to find time-tested roses.

Late spring and early summer, the peak of rose season, is the time for such a hunt, and the town cemetery is a good starting point. It was the custom a century ago to plant mother's favorite flower beside her grave, and that was usually a rose. Since gravesites, unlike gardens, don't pass from owner to owner and so are not relandscaped every generation, the rosebushes can grow there undisturbed—and the date on the headstone offers a clue to the age of the flower.

Other places to look are ethnic enclaves—Pennsylvania Dutch communities, for example, whose conservatism has protected old roses from replacement. In the South, the older black neighborhoods are often the best hunting grounds—roses were a special enthusiasm of the women there, many of whom were known locally for their phenomenal skill in the garden. Bypassed rural areas also furnish many finds. I've never seen a display to match the roses growing in the ghost towns of California's gold rush country, and the abandoned farms of upstate New York and New England have furnished my garden with a choice, if more limited, selection. The roses I've discovered on trips to these areas have varied tremendously in appearance, but they all agree in one respect: They are survivors. Time has weeded out the weaklings.

Identifying your finds will be the next step in introducing these traditional roses into your garden. Botanical keys, indexes of garden roses classified by physical characteristics, are available from horticultural libraries, but personally I find them incomprehensible. Far easier, and more enjoyable too, is to visit a labelled collection of antique roses such as you'll find in the Cranford Rose Garden at Brooklyn Botanic Garden. There you can match your finds, at least approximately, with the cultivars on display. Or contact the experts at the Heritage Rose Group*. With regional chapters covering every part of the country, this fellowship of old-rose fanciers can direct you to someone knowledgeable about the older roses in your area, as well as information about where they can be purchased. Modest annual dues which include the cost of a quarterly

A close-up view of 'Souvenir de la Malmaisson' showing the pale pink flowers which appear intermittently until frost.

newsletter make membership in this organization an outstanding bargain.

Even the most cursory foray into old rose identification is intoxicating, since it reveals the startling selection of blossoms cultivated by cottage gardeners of our great-grandparents' day. Currently, a half dozen giant concerns supply virtually all our roses, and they rarely bother with anything besides hybrid teas and floribundas. The catalogs of a century ago, however, listed a dozen or more classes, each one different in the typical form of the

'Archduke Charles' is a China rose that combines well with other garden plants. Here it complements the planting in front of the house.

flowers, the season of bloom and in its regional adaptations. What's more, since there were hundreds of nurserymen hybridizing their own roses, the gardener then had his choice of thousands of cultivars. From this host, I've chosen the following representative sample, a handful of the many that I've found in cottage gardens around the country:

'Tuscany Superb'—This cultivar has been naturalized in America's cottage gardens for more than a century. It is a rose of the ancient French gallica class. Wine-colored blossoms with a knot of golden threads at their centers adorn this shrub for three or four weeks in early summer; the three- to four-foot tall canes are as winter hardy as an oak.

'Paul Neyron'—As much as seven inches across, this cultivar's pink flowers are among the largest and the most fragrant of any garden rose. A member of the hybrid perpetual class, 'Paul Neyron' is a star performer in cold climates, blooming heavily in early summer and again occasionally through late fall.

'Hippolyte'—Soft violet in color, the compact flowers of this cultivar arrange their petals in a tight, plump spiral around a central "button eye," with an effect like that of an overstuffed cushion. Almost thornless, this gallica rose raises arching branches six feet high and is equally at home in the foothills of California's Sierra Nevadas or in a Northeastern front yard. Blooms for a three- to four-week period from late spring into early summer.

'Souvenir de la Malmaison'—Named in memory of the Empress Josephine's rose garden, this is a bourbon rose, a representative of one of the oldest classes of reblooming roses. After a heavy June flowering it continues producing its broad, pale pink flowers intermittently until frost. Described as "quartered" by rosarians, these blossoms marshal their petals in a cross-shaped pattern. This adaptable rose

withstands northern winters or southern summers with equal aplomb.

'Musk Rose'—A climbing rose whose uniquely spicy perfume has made it a favorite since Shakespeare's time, the musk came to America with the first colonists. A useful complement to the early summer roses, the musk flowers at summer's end, bearing generous clusters of small, five-petalled white blossoms well into September. Hardy north or south.

'Common Moss'—This rose's name derives from the thick growth of resinous green glands that encrusts the flower buds—they really do appear overgrown with an aromatic moss. This feature, together with the fine prickles that sheathe the branches and a shiny green foliage, make this an attractive shrub even when it is not sporting its wheels of clear pink petals. Four to five feet tall, the common moss generally proves frost proof as far north as Boston.

'Old Blush'—A China rose that was brought back to Europe by a Swedish ship's doctor in 1752, this forms a dense shrub as much as six feet tall with semi-double, blush-pink flowers shaped like architectural rosettes. Though the blossoms are nearly scentless, they do rebloom throughout the warm weather. A rose for southern climates, 'Old Blush' is not reliably winter hardy north of Philadelphia but is nearly impervious to heat, humidity and drought. I've seen specimens in central Texas that were flourishing after 50 years of neglect.

'Hermosa'—Another China rose, this one sports globe-shaped, fragrant blossoms of lilac-pink. After a springtime flush of flowers, 'Hermosa' reblooms sparingly through the summer, mounting a renewed display with the arrival of autumn's cool, moist weather. Probably the most common rose of California's gold rush country, this cultivar will tolerate some frost but not the severe cold of northern winters.

'Champneys' Pink Cluster'—This climber was introduced by a South Carolina rice planter in 1811. It is one of the first garden roses bred in the United States. The clusters of deep, rose-pink buds open to offer bouquets of small but double, blush-colored, very fragrant flowers. Not hardy north of Philadelphia.

'Marie Van Houtte'—A tea rose, so-called because older roses of this class do have a refreshing, oolonglike fragrance. The very double blossoms nod as if too heavy for their stems; the pale yellow petals are tipped with pink. Disease-, insect- and heat-resistant, this reblooming rose is a champion in the South, but not hardy in the North.

As may be gathered from these descriptions, old roses, with the exception of the tea roses, are all, to a greater or lesser degree, seasonal. That is, they produce a heavy flush of bloom at one season, generally in late spring or early summer, and then rebloom sparingly or not at all. This does not mean that their display is less generous. A typical hybrid perpetual yields 95 percent of its bloom in June and July, but in that relatively brief period, it bears more blossoms than the average hybrid tea does over the course of an entire summer and fall.

Cottage gardeners didn't expect their roses to be "everblooming," but many modern gardeners can't abide a seasonal rose. Fortunately, David Austin, an English nurseryman, has recently introduced a happy compromise: the new hybrids he calls his "English Roses." Similar in form and fragrance to the old roses, they pace their flowering like a hybrid tea, producing a steady succession of flowers throughout the growing season.**

Having chosen your roses, how do you incorporate them into the garden in an authentic manner? Probably it was due to a lack of space, but cottage gardeners didn't segregate their roses into a bed of their own. Instead, they wove the roses right into the tapestry of flowers, vegetables and herbs with which they covered their plots. Gallica roses, for example, a class whose petals were supposed to increase in fragrance as they dried and so were favored for potpourris, cottagers commonly planted among the culinary herbs outside the kitchen door.

Because the old-time roses generally make denser, handsomer shrubs than the twiggy hybrid teas, they work well as accents in a flower border. I've seen the crimson blossoms of China rose 'Fabvier' pose an elegant contrast to the silvered foliage of lamb's-ears (*Stachys byzantina*), and the scarlet flowers of the 'Apothecary Rose' (*Rosa gallica officinalis*—a centuries-old source, as the name suggests, of herbal remedies) combine in a vivid bouquet with the little, daisylike blossoms of feverfew (*Chrysanthemum parthenium*). Some of the cottagers' roses even serve as foliage plants. The canes and foliage of the red-leaf rose (*Rosa rubrifolia*), for example, are colored a rich maroon, furnishing a colorful display long after the shrub's small pink flowers have finished their spring show.

Often, cottage gardeners trained the roses on simple trellises to use them as a structural element within the garden—an arch of roses might shelter the front gate and a curtain of roses shade the porch. But the most striking effect, one that is easily copied, usually came only after a garden was abandoned. A climbing rose adjacent to a tree might take advantage of the caretaker's absence to climb up the trunk and into the branches. The garlands of flowers such a survivor flaunts are one of the most spectacular sights of a rose-explorer's spring. ❖

* *Northeast coordinator of Heritage Rose Group is Lily Shohan, R. D. 1, Box 228, Clinton Corners, NY 12514.*
** *English Roses—These remarkable new roses are available from Wayside Gardens, Hodges, SC 29695 and Pickering Nurseries, 670 Kingston Rd., Pickering, Ontario, Canada L1V 1A6.*

Cottage Garden Ornament

A cement hen with her chicks parades across the lawn. True yard art often makes no statement, has no pretenses. The oaks and privet are pruned into smooth balls and tight hedges.

Felder Rushing

Cottage gardens, especially rural ones, have always had some type of ornament to "carry things through" from season to season. Sometimes serious works of art, sometimes castoff *objets trouve*, there are no universally loved styles of "yard art."

True yard art often makes no statement, has no pretenses. It exists only for the pleasure of the gardener and his or her muse. Usually it is a one-of-a-kind. It is even hard to draw conclusions about origins of some art—it may transcend racial and economic lines.

There is a proud difference, when it comes to yard art, between "tacky" and gaudy. A gaudy object is done on purpose, and its owner is given a bit of tacit respect for his efforts. *Tacky* is when he just doesn't know any better, bless his heart.

After screening out all the unoriginal, manufactured plastic doo-dads (whirling windmills, flamingos, sleeping sombreros), all cut-out plywood figures of bent-over gardeners (fanny shots), and a plethora of birdbaths, cement chickens and the like, there remains a fascinating assortment of original ideas. 🝲

Above: *This old millstone makes a perfect foil in the herb and perennial garden. The color and texture also add interest to the scene.*

Right: *Pink plastic flamingos seem to be enjoying a resurgence in popularity.*

Below: *Here is the Bayou chair—the quintessential, universal Southern yard adornment which usually presents itself under several coats of paint, much of it chipped.*

Celia Thaxter's Island Garden

Virginia Chisholm

Celia Thaxter was photographed in her garden on Appledore Island. She enjoyed cutting flowers from her garden for the house and often arose early in the morning to spend time working there.

Perhaps one of the smallest and loveliest cottage gardens was begun over a hundred years ago by Celia Thaxter (1835-1894) on Appledore Island. Appledore Island is one of the nine rugged islands that make up the Isles of Shoals located six miles off the coast of New Hampshire.

Celia Thaxter grew up on these islands. Her father, Thomas Laighton, built the first of the huge resort hotels that would eventually line the east coast of Appledore Island. When Celia was 16 she married Levi Thaxter who was 12 years her senior. Levi was an intellectual dreamer who relied on his father, a Boston banker, to support him, his wife and their three sons. Levi's father gave them a house just outside Boston where Celia was expected to do everything from milking the cow to making their clothes. In order to cope with the drudgery, Celia began to compose poetry as she worked. Her first poem, "Landlocked," was published in *The Atlantic Monthly* and was an immediate

Virginia Chisholm is an artist and teacher turned gardener. She restored the gardens at Hamilton House, South Berwick, Maine, for The Society for the Preservation of New England Antiquities. She is chairman of The Moffatt-Ladd House garden in Portsmouth, New Hampshire, owned by The National Society of The Colonial Dames of America in New Hampshire, and she is director of Celia Thaxter's Garden on Appledore Island, the Isles of Shoals. All of these gardens are open to the public.

This is Appledore House which burned in 1914, destroying Celia's cottage in the blaze. The garden was re-established in 1970 on its original site in front of the old foundation.

success. Realizing that poetry could bring in needed income, she wrote for every magazine she could, and soon was very well known. The poems were about the sea and the islands she loved so much.

Her marriage ended when Levi became ill and was advised by his doctors to go south. Levi moved, taking with him the two younger boys. Celia returned to Appledore with her eldest son Karl to care for her ailing mother. She would remain on the island for the rest of her life, except for a six-month tour of Europe and winters spent in Portsmouth, New Hampshire, or Boston. This was the most productive time of her life. Several books of her poetry were published, and one book of prose about the Isles of Shoals. Celia also discovered she could paint, and she decorated one-hundred-piece sets of china with her favorite flowers to augment her small income.

By this time the hotel had grown under the management of her brothers and could sleep 500 and seat 900 in the dining room. People came by the boatful to see the islands and Celia. When she and Levi were living near Boston, Charles Fields, the publisher of *The Atlantic Monthly*, and his wife Annie became close friends, and through them their coterie of intelligentsia came to know Celia and followed her to Appledore Island summer after summer. The visitors included James Russell Lowell, William Hawthorne, William Dean Howells, Henry Ward Beecher, Harriet Beecher Stowe, Samuel Longfellow, Richard Henry Dana, John Greenleaf Whittier, Sara Orne Jewett, Ole Bull, William Morris Hunt, Ross Turner, Albert Thompson Bricher and Childe Hassam.

Celia eventually inherited her mother's cottage. During the summers, her parlor became like the salons in Europe with daily concerts and readings. In order to reach Celia's parlor, a guest had to pass through the gate and her garden, and as Celia's parlor became famous, so did her garden.

Her friends prevailed upon her to write a book about her garden, but she thought this ridiculous. "It's only a cutting garden, a jumble of flowers." It was a cutting garden, for she enjoyed arranging the flowers for her parlor as much as she enjoyed growing them. In the last years of her life, encouraged by Sara Orne Jewett, Celia wrote "An Island Garden." It is a charming book written in the flowery style of the era and illustrated by Childe Hassam. To those who wish to restore or create a garden of this period, this book is a treasure.

Celia's book takes you through the gardening year in this small 15- by 50-foot garden surrounded by a gray fence to protect it from the strong prevailing winds. A narrow continuous bed runs just inside the fence and nine small raised beds make up the center section. She included a diagram and planting scheme, but in reading the book one realizes that she did not always stick to the same plan. She liked to start her own seeds so the garden is mostly annuals. Celia planted her seeds early in wooden flats kept in south-facing windows. Difficult varieties she started in eggshells. She certainly would approve of the peat pots and plastic trays of today.

There are pages of descriptions of the flowers she grew, as well as the wild flowers on the island. Most of the flowers are listed only by their common names: hollyhocks, marigolds, stock, zinnia, china asters, single dahlias, sunflowers, sweet william, balsam, poppies (California and especially shirleys), sweet peas, tuberous begonias, larkspur, *Phlox drummondii* and foxglove to name a few. She had just a few perennials, a red peony, white phlox; Scotch, rugosa, polyantha, damask and hybrid perpetual roses; *Lilium candidum*, yellow and orange day lilies and delphinium. Many vines were trained up and over the porch to provide much needed shade:

The garden in early fall is a blaze of color. There are hollyhocks, marigolds, stock, zinnia, asters, sunflowers, balsam and many other familiar garden flowers of yesteryear.

The garden is planted according to Celia's original plan. Some of the old varieties have been hard to find as flowers go in and out of style.

Japanese hops, wisteria, nasturtium, clematis, honeysuckle, akebia and morning-glory. The same Japanese hops that were used to make beer for the hotel still twine over the back fence of the garden. Shirley poppies were her favorites and these she planted in succession so they could be enjoyed all summer.

Celia rose to work in her garden at four in the morning. This must have been the only time she could be by herself and enjoy the early morning and the flowers she loved so much. Celia died in 1894 just after *An Island Garden* was published. She is buried on Appledore Island with the Laightons. The Appledore House burned in 1914, destroying Celia's cottage in the blaze.

Appledore Island remained deserted until the 1970s when the Shoals Marine Laboratory, a summer school of marine biology run jointly by Cornell University and the University of New Hampshire, was begun by Dr. John Kingsbury. Dr. Kingsbury re-established Celia's garden on its original site, in front of the foundation of her cottage. Since his retirement, I maintain the garden with the help of the

Rye Garden Club. The flowers are grown by the Thompson School of the University of New Hampshire and brought to the island at the end of May to be planted.

In the beginning it was difficult to find seeds of some of the old-fashioned flowers that had not been dwarfed, doubled or so developed that they lost their scent. Now, with the great interest in restoring old gardens, the old varieties of seeds are reappearing. We still cannot find "tall" single dahlias, picotee pinks (*Dianthus*) and some of Celia's roses. The garden is planted according to her diagram, but as the summer goes on, plants are supplemented with those she writes about but does not include in the diagram. It may seem surprising, but flowers go out of style just like clothing. Visitors to the garden are often surprised by the number of flowers they have never seen before. The helianthus, Celia's sunflowers, *Phlox drummondii,* calliopsis, lavatera, venidium, hesperis, crimson flax, mignonette and viscaria that Celia used to illustrate her books are not common today.

Celia planted many white flowers in the garden because she thought they looked lovely in the moonlight. She had a tall white opium poppy she called "The Bride," white petunias, white phlox and white mignonette. Another white plant was the clematis or traveller's-joy (*Clematis vitalba*), which is like the *C. paniculata* that blooms in September. The clematis is no longer in the garden, but seeded over the island by the birds. Its fragrance led us to it, but we have not been successful in reproducing the plant because most of it grows in the most enormous patch of poison ivy one could imagine.

Celia had no problem with water because there was a large reservoir and rain water was collected from the roofs, but then there were no gulls to pollute the water. Now, in order to conserve water from the one well on the island, there is a low sprinkler system with a timer on the center beds.

We have been improving the soil over the years in the same way Celia did, with seaweed, manure and the compost that we ask visitors to bring when they come to the garden. We also keep two compost piles in the corners of the cottage foundation.

Our greatest problem, other than the gulls pulling out every white flower, are the muskrats. We don't have the slugs or sparrows that plagued Celia, but she didn't have gulls or muskrats. The muskrats are a true pest. Last year they broke into the garden three times before we could install new, stronger wire around the bottom of the wooden fence. Naturally, the more special the plant, the faster the muskrats ate it.

Some people who visit are vastly disappointed in this delightful little jewel on this harsh rugged island. Many expect a restored English garden with yew hedges. Certainly Childe Hassam's illustrations in Celia's book might lead one to that conclusion. It is a charming garden, and the colors are brilliant as they so often are on the coast. The interest in the garden is amazing. People come by ferry, by cruise ships and in their own boats. The garden is open from July through Labor Day by permission only, and permission can be obtained by calling the Shoals Marine Laboratory at Cornell University (607-225-3717) or at the island (603-964-9011). The Isles of Shoals Steamship Co. in Portsmouth, New Hampshire, runs a ferry to Star Island, and from there a Boston Whaler will take you across Gosport Harbor to Appledore Island.

It is a delightful day trip. The ferry leaves at 11:00 a.m. from Portsmouth and the return trip leaves Star Island at 3:00 p.m. Appledore Island is rugged and, if you're dressed for hiking and have picnic in hand, there is a lot to explore.

Celia's book *An Island Garden*, with an introduction by Dr. Kingsbury can be purchased through the Shoals Marine Laboratory, G-14-E, Stimson Hall, Cornell

University, Ithaca, NY 14853. Other books about Celia and the Islands are also available. ✒

Celia Thaxter's Plant List

Alcea rosea	hollyhock	Single & double mix
Aster		'Pastelle' mix China
Aquilegia vulgaris	columbine	
Impatiens balsamina	balsam	mix
Begonia		tuberous
Campanula medium	cup-and-saucer	mix
Cleome	spider flower	mix
Cheiranthus cheiri	wallflower	mix
Coreopsis tinctoria	calliopsis	
Coreopsis		donated seeds
Centaurea cyanus	bachelor's-button	
Cosmos		'Sensation' mix
Dahlia		singles only
Delphinium		Pacific
Dianthus barbatus	sweet william	
D. deltoides	maiden pinks	
Digitalis purpurea	foxglove	
Gaillardia		
Helianthus	sunflower	donated from an old garden
Hesperis	sweet rocket	donated from an old garden
Iberis	candytuft	mix
Ipomoea	morning-glory	'Heavenly Blue'
Lathyrus odoratus	sweet pea	climbing mix
Consolida ambigua	larkspur	'Imperial Blue'
Lavatera trimestris		'Mont Blanc'
Lychnis viscaria	rose campion	
Nicotiana	flowering tobacco	mix
Nigella	love-in-the-mist	
Pelargonium	geranium	
Phlox drummondii	drummond phlox	dwarf mix
Petunia		white single
Penstemon	beard-tongue	mix
Reseda	mignonette	white
Tagetes	marigold	orange & yellow
Tropaeolum	nasturtium	mix
Verbena officinalis	vervain	
Viola odorata	pansy	
Zinnia		mix

One waterlily (*Nymphaea*) in a tub
In 1989 some 80 trays of seedlings went into this garden.

This is a view of the garden from the vantage point of what would have been the old porch. The arbor provides a nice structural element.

Two Urban Cottage Gardens in the Rockies

Panayoti Kelaidis

Above: *The Proctor-Macke garden is really three gardens in one. This century-old brick brownstone is around the corner from Rob's and Dave's first garden. The new garden is planted with cool-loving plants that need only a half day's sun.*

Right: *Roses and nicotiana complement each other nicely in the garden beside the century-old brick brownstone.*

Photos by Rob Proctor

The Rocky Mountains usually summon up images of lofty, snow-covered mountains, or perhaps flowery alpine meadows reflected in pristine montane lakes. While many people come to this region because of the recreational opportunities that mountains provide, residents have gradually discovered that gardening with flowers here offers gratifying rewards. The intense, high altitude sun and crisp mountain air may present obstacles to growing delicate broadleaf evergreens, but these conditions bring out the best in most traditional garden flowers. Indeed, many stalwart plants of cottage gardens, such as McKana columbines, coralbells, gaillardias and penstemons are *bona fide* Rocky Mountain wildflowers that are known and loved in gardens everywhere. Exotics such as Siberian and German irises, old-fashioned shrub roses, butter-and-eggs (*Linaria vulgaris*) and even peonies will persist for generations around old homesteads and ghost towns to remind us that gardening does have a

history in this relatively youthful part of our country.

It is important for gardeners to realize that there are really two very different climatic regions that coexist and sometimes overlap in the Rockies: the high country (roughly above 6000 feet) where the frost-free season is very short and daytime temperatures rarely exceed 80 degrees F in the summer months, and the lowlands (sometimes called the high plains) at altitudes below 6000 feet. Practically all traditional garden perennials thrive at higher elevations, and bloom much longer and more vividly than in warmer climates. Annuals, though popular, are something of a luxury in areas with a frost-free season only a few weeks long! Below 6000 feet, heat and summer drought are limiting factors. Traditional garden plants need frequent irrigation and some shade to do their best. Many unusual perennials from drier climates, like the American Southwest, Western and Central Asia, the Mediterranean basin and South Africa are being introduced and promise a sophisticated new garden palette for this region. And many annuals perform magnificently for months on end.

The dichotomy of high country and lowlands is beautifully illustrated by visiting a few of the many cottage gardens that have grown up in this region recently. Two of the most influential cottage gardens are Rob Proctor's and David Macke's Capitol Hill extravaganza in the heart of Denver at a mere mile of elevation, and the Bay Street Company storefront garden at 9600 feet in Breckenridge, Colorado. Breckenridge is a historic mining town that has tremendous summer tourist traffic and a famous winter ski resort. Over the years, thousands of Colorado residents and "out of staters" have driven past the Bay Street Company and seen a cornucopia of color in the summer months. The Proctor-Macke garden is best known through Rob Proctor's

prolific writing in recent years, as well as his lectures and classes which have made him the pre-eminent spokesman for creative gardening in this region.

Cottage gardens are conventionally associated with rural, or at least sparsely populated, settings where a meadow or farmyard can be glimpsed beyond the flowery verge. Here are two gardens, one in the heart of a mountain village, and the other less than a mile from the Capitol building of the largest metropolis of the Rocky Mountain region, which demonstrate the rich possibilities in this traditional but ever popular style of gardening.

The Proctor-Macke Garden

The Proctor-Macke garden is really three gardens in one. It began as an attempt to rehabilitate the courtyard of a historic apartment complex where Rob and David lived. The dusty courtyard was little more than a graveyard of cement clothesline bases and pitiful turf when the occupants of a dozen units banded together to "add a little color." In two years the edges of the commons had been double dug and filled with a riot of color. Herbs, annuals, perennials and the beginning of Rob's lily collection jostled for space and attention. The hot northwest corner of the courtyard was planted with heat-tolerant natives and Mediterraneans: a giant fountain of *Gaura lindheimeri* blossoms from early summer to frost. Lamb's-ear (*Stachys byzantina*) and coralbells (*Heuchera*) combine in a silver and scarlet *leit motif* which is echoed in all the warm corners of the garden. To the south, under a gnarled, ancient box elder tree (*Acer negundo*), a bench rests on a flagstone semicircular patio edged with white impatiens which overlooks the grassy courtyard surrounded by a kaleidoscopic border of color. Every apartment unit has a ringside view, and vacancies (which occur rarely in this complex, despite Denver's sluggish economy) do not last very long. In the shade around the bench woodland flowers and shade-loving perennials create a tapestry. Here wild gingers and woodruff carpet the ground, with various ferns and Asiatic lilies rising behind them. Astilbe and aruncus with their filigree foliage, anemones and snowdrops, hellebores, lobelias, many kinds of primroses, hostas and jack-in-the-pulpits—plants not usually associated with the Rockies—thrive here given a little shade and irrigation.

Turning the corner and entering the first of many gates brings one to the backyard of a century-old brick brownstone that fortuitously was put up for sale when Rob and Dave were in the market for a house. The theme of this protected space is a sort of cottage/knot garden featuring cool-loving plants that need only a half day's sun and shaded roots. Some eight or ten planting beds defined by neat grassy paths contain a vast collection of perennials intermingled with Rob's special passion: Asiatic and woodland lilies. Here dozens of species lilies and special hybrids are combined with complementary ground covers that keep their roots cool and provide interest when the lilies' giant goblets are not on display. A six-foot fence was built to mask the adjacent property, a quarter acre of hopelessly trashy, weedy ground begging for attention. In time, this lot also proved an irresistible temptation. The neighborhood church, which owned the lot, had no plans for this eyesore, so like manifest destiny, the cottage garden continued to expand.

This third part of the triptych came to being only in 1987 when tons of debris and weeds were removed and the thin clay was enriched a bit to accommodate a series of gardens in this quintessential urban setting: to the south a parking lot, to the west a picket fence and street, to the north the Macke/Proctor homestead, to the east an alleyway. A border of annuals, perennials and shrubs, designed to soften fence lines, winds in a horseshoe shape around the entire property. Flower color begins with cool blues and lavenders at the southwest corner, progressing through white and pastel pinks and mauves to purpler and finally redder tones in its very center, heating up to a riot of hot yellows, oranges and scarlets along the eastern border where, even on overcast summer days, most visitors get noticeably agitated. The center of the garden consists of a bountiful vegetable garden and formal herb garden built around an emblematic pineapple sculpture and a trellis.

Practically the entire palette of classic annuals and perennials can be found in one or another of the three parts of this Denver garden: a mass of *Coreopsis verticillata* 'Moonbeam' drifting beneath a mound of albino *Echinacea purpurea* backed by a diaphanous mass of baby's-breath. Clumps of double feverfew in eerie white form an edging to pastel yellow, upright lilies with dark red roses clambering behind. Undulating mats of bright, white snow-on-the-mountain (*Cerastium tomentosum*) alternate with chalk pink *Saponaria ocymoides* in early summer. Yellow and white trumpet lilies are bordered with monarda and a riot of purple, pale yellow and white dwarf perennials along the path to the house. California poppies edge a mass of blue flax in June. These and a hundred more vignettes through the entire growing season have convinced local gardeners of the endless delights and possibilities of traditional flower gardens in the Rocky Mountains. This garden is a testament to the evocative power of the cottage garden—particularly in the heart of a metropolis.

Breckenridge

Breckenridge is far removed psychologically from urban Denver, but this small town situated in the Blue River Valley of Summit County, Colorado, has been built up considerably in the last two decades. The Victorian storefronts along Main

Some eight or ten planting beds defined by neat grassy paths contain a vast collection of perennials intermingled with Rob's special passion: Asiatic and woodland lilies.

Street have been lovingly restored and painted festive colors, and like many Rocky Mountain tourist towns, the number of visitors seems to be related directly to the number of hanging baskets and flowers lavished on the town. While Vail has its window boxes and Winter Park its giant planters, Breckenridge has provided a continuous strip of planting beds along both sides of the street, which are variously planted with wildflowers, annuals, shrubs and even trees.

One corner store in the center of town has a particularly generous strip of land almost 20 feet deep from the street to the recessed storefront. The Bay Street Com-

Right: *A lovely mass of iris blooms beside a clump of carnations, providing an interesting accent as well as soft color.*

Below: *The white wicker chairs invite guests to sit and enjoy the lush beauty of the Proctor-Macke garden. The garden is a lovely retreat from the city streets.*

pany, a gift shop, has been owned by Dodie Bingham for ten years. Long an avid gardener, Dodie boasts that she spends her entire advertising budget on plants, a sentiment that inspires local nurserymen to contemplate her canonization. Perennials and would-be annuals such as larkspur and poppies were planted thickly from the very start. Frost can occur in any month (the frost-free season is less than a month most years), and most other businesses don't plant their annuals until well into June. But at the Bay Street Company, the flowering season starts as early as April with the first crocuses, daffodils and even violas, which reveal their alpine origins by being thoroughly perennial here. The procession of color builds quickly in May, and by June the garden is in glorious peak: columbines, lupines, geraniums, shasta daisies, iceland poppies and a jungle of traditional garden plants bloom in top form (with a little judicious dead-heading) the entire summer season. They are joined by tree-sized delphiniums, a large collection of true lilies and virtually the entire pageant of perennials that can be found in most garden books, as well as a few local wildflowers introduced from the lush meadows hereabouts. Most annuals are cut down by the first frosts late in August or early September, but many perennials in this garden progress well into October most years, proving just how important they really are to horticulture in extreme climatic situations.

Both the Proctor-Macke garden and the Bay Street Company garden share qualities associated with most cottage gardens: an intimate setting filled with lush plants that produce a mass of color for the entire growing season. Both gardens are eclectic: Wildflowers, unusual and well-known annuals, perennials, even vegetables are combined under trees and among shrubs to create a panorama of color through the season. The mountain garden at Breckenridge evokes and intensifies the image of flowery meadows and woodlands that can be found nearby. The city garden is much larger, consisting of a dozen or more discrete units, each of which has its own theme for color, culture and texture. Visitors to either garden are convinced not only of the rich possibilities in cottage gardening, but in the promise of horticulture a mile or two up in the sky.

Ten Cottage Garden Plants from the Rockies

Aquilegia caerulea—This parent of most garden hybrid columbines is always worth growing in its own right, since no hybrid can approach the luminous blue and white of the wild forms. I find the subtle but strong lavender fragrance of the wild species enchanting. Several breeders have begun to select columbines for resistance to leaf miners and heat tolerance as well as superior traits of color and form. Pure colored strains are also being marketed.

Erigeron speciosus—The Aspen daisy has been a popular garden plant in Europe for over a century. Local gardeners are beginning to examine the huge clan of fleabane daisies and asters that are responsible for making at least one Englishman suggest the Rockies be renamed the Daisy Chain. *E. speciosus* is particularly large and lush. *E. peregrinus* is neater and much deeper in flower color.

Eustoma grandiflorum—As with so many native plants, the tulip gentian has had to go abroad (in this case, Japan) to be gussied up a bit in order to be accepted back in the United States. The Japanese selected for sumptuous color and flower size at the expense of longevity. Perhaps they employed Texan rather than more northerly germ plasm. Reliably perennial tulip gentians occur throughout Wyoming, Colorado and Nebraska in white, deep purple and lavender phases. Few native plants bloom for a longer season in the wild or in the garden, and fewer still have such a large and showy flower.

Heuchera sanguinea—Not many people realize that coralbells originated in the southern fringes of the Rockies of New Mexico, Arizona and Chihuahua. Despite their southerly origin, they are indestructibly hardy throughout the Northern Hemisphere, tolerating almost any soil, moisture regime and exposure.

Mertensia ciliata—Virginia bluebells (*M. virginica*) are well known and loved in woodland gardens. They behave much like bulbs, popping up early in spring and disappearing just as promptly. Only a few gardens have introduced Western chiming bells (*M. ciliata*), but these tall, much more substantial perennials have proven to have a very long bloom season and tolerance of many soils and exposures, promising a bright future in gardens. *Mertensia* is a genus largely centered in the Rockies.

Oenothera caespitosa—Only a handful of yellow evening primroses have appeared in the general nursery trade. Western gardeners are mostly familiar with this shimmering white, stemless evening primrose that occurs over much of the dry lowlands up to montane elevations throughout the West. Not only are the flowers huge, but intensely fragrant. Some forms have crinkly, hairy foliage that suggests the frosting on wedding cakes, while other forms can be quite weedy with numerous, unwelcome underground runners. The better forms are fine edgings for cottage gardens.

Oxytropis sericea and *O. lambertii*—Few wildflower spectacles exceed the brilliance of Western landscapes when the locoweeds are at their peak. White loco (*O. sericea*) is very easily grown from seed and can persist for five years or more in a sunny border. The vivid magenta of *O. lambertii* upsets delicate tastes, but delights children and extroverts. It needs better drainage or a dry spot to prove perennial under garden conditions.

Penstemon pinifolius—This plant grows over much the same range as *Heuchera*, has a similarly wide tolerance, and shares coralbells' long bloom season. The colorful Mexican phloxes are promising a similar bright future.

Penstemon strictus 'Bandera'—In the Western mountains, three or four dozen species of penstemons form tall, spikelike inflorescences of dazzling cobalt or gentian blue. Only one, so far, has been selected for uniformity, promptness of germination and tolerance of a wide range of soils and moisture conditions: 'Bandera' is a superlative border plant with bright blue color that rivals *Meconopsis* (blue poppies) and gentians in vividness. Many frustrated gardeners struggle to grow blue poppies while ignoring much more easily accommodated penstemons that are every bit as pure and dazzling in their blues.

Yucca harrimaniae—Yuccas were among Gertrude Jekyll's favorite plants for architectural effect in the garden. The southeastern species are admittedly large and ponderous in a border. Several dwarf western species make lively accents for a warm garden, and this Great Basin species has narrow spikes of a vivid white in late spring that strike a distinctive chord during that busy season.

Zauschneria californica latifolia and *Z. garrettii*—The California fuchsias are neither fuchsias nor restricted to California. Two of the showiest species occur in the southern and middle Rockies. *Z. garrettii* from Utah, Idaho and Wyoming makes compact green mats with bright red-orange trumpets throughout the summer season. It is unquestionably the earliest, hardiest and most adaptable member of the genus. *Z. californica latifolia* grows three to four feet tall and is obscured by deep orange trumpets from August to frost. In cold climates it should be planted in spring, and given lots of room to make a veritable burning bush in a year or two of growth. ❀

Top: *The hot colors combine to attract the eye —the original intent was to "add a little color."*

Photos by Rob Proctor

Bottom: *Coral bells (Heuchera) and lamb's-ear combine in a silver and scarlet* leitmotif *which is echoed in all the warm corners of the gardens such as the above.*

Cottage Garden Plants for the Piedmont

Nancy Goodwin

Cottage gardening appeals to everyone who loves growing plants. There is a delicious feeling of escape from one's everyday surroundings when standing in the midst of informal masses of flowers. Although we may become sophisticated in our approach to color, designing monochromatic beds or ones that are planned on graph paper to achieve a perfect balance of color and form, many "well-planned" gardens never achieve the glorious feeling of reveling in the plants the way a cottage garden does.

Many of the best gardens in the South consist of plants handed down from friend to friend, from parents to their children or from one cottage garden to another. That is how so many of the old-fashioned names persist, and how new ones carry meanings beyond the plants themselves. In my own garden I cherish Fanny's aster from an unknown gardener in South Caro-

Photos by Elvin McDonald

Many cottage gardens in the South are just outside the back door with herbs, vegetables and flowers grown in perfect harmony. Here Ocimum basilicum *'Spicy Globe' and 'Dark Opal'.*

Colorful nasturtiums, Tropaeolum majus, *surround leafy green lettuce in a charming arrangement. Simple combinations in the garden are often the most effective.*

lina, and there are old primulas which have competed with grass and survived neglect during droughts, but which have no recognized name. These are the kinds of plants that form the basis of most cottage gardens. To see the same plants in practically every garden in old towns indicates the quality of friendships there.

Many cottage gardens in the South are just outside the back door where vegetables and flowers are grown in perfect harmony without careful consideration of

Nancy Goodwin started Montrose Nursery in Hillsborough, North Carolina, in 1984. The original idea was to specialize in cyclamens, but the list rapidly expanded to include many perennials. Nancy and her husband moved into their first house in 1963, and she's spent every minute in the garden ever since.

eja montana, spreads in a civilized way and is attractive and edible all year. The dark purple or green leaved forms of basil, *Ocimum basilicum,* are superb foliage plants, and holy basil, *O. sanctum,* has a haunting fragrance. Fennel, especially the purple leaved one, *Foeniculum vulgare* 'Rubrum', is a fine cottage plant, better as an ornament than for eating. There are many oreganos available for such gardens. Two are the golden leaved *Origanum vulgare* 'Aureum' which provides an excellent base for dark flowers or foliage, and the charming *O. pulchellum* with its drooping sprays of pink flowers coming out from large, green bracts.

Shrubs provide structure throughout winter and put perennials and annuals into perspective. Excellent ones for this region include *Spiraea thunbergii* which blooms with fragrant, single, white flowers after any mild spell from November through March. Sweet breath of spring, *Lonicera fragrantissima,* has associations for anyone who has lived near it. The small creamy white flowers are fragrant enough to bring back all of the memories of childhood and more. January jasmine, *Jasminum nudiflorum,* is a plant found in many old gardens. The buds tipped with red beg to be brought inside and respond to a little warmth by opening their lovely yellow flowers. Sweet betsy or sweetshrub, *Calycanthus floridus,* is a native shrub with reddish-brown flowers announced by their bananalike fragrance. It is a good plant for shade or part sun. Roses are wonderful in a cottage garden, but there is a stiffness about the hybrid teas that eliminates them from my list. Instead, choose 'New Dawn', 'Mermaid' or 'Silver Moon' to cover large areas, or 'Blanc Double de Coubert' and 'Frau Dagmar Hastrup' for constant bloom without spraying.

To plan a garden so that it doesn't look planned is a difficult task, for it cannot thrive on benign neglect. The more aggressive plants will destroy their neighbors. A selective process of culling out the less desirable colors and forms while allowing an abundance of growth of those annuals, perennials and bulbs which are acceptable is necessary to achieve the balance desired. As in all interesting gardens, this one will be different every year.

Top: Phlox divaricata *has a place in the cottage gardens of the Southeast. Plants must be well tended but given the freedom to spread.*

Bottom: *'Purple Ruffles' basil is a superb foliage plant. It combines interesting foliage with wonderful flavor.*

Peonies are a must in all cottage gardens—especially the ones that are old fashioned, floppy and fragrant.

Cottage Garden Plants

Shrubs:

*Calycanthus**	Carolina sweet shrub
Caryopteris	bluemist, bluebeard
Clethra alnifolia	summersweet, sweet pepperbush
*Daphne**	
Euonymus americana	strawberry bush, hearts a bustin'
Exochorda	pearlbush
*Hamamelis**	witch hazel
Hibiscus mutabilis	Confederate rose
Hibiscus syriacus	rose-of-sharon
Hydrangea	
Juniperus	
Kerria	
Ligustrum	crape myrtle
*Lonicera fragrantissima**	honeysuckle
*Philadelphus**	mock orange
Poncirus trifoliata	hardy orange, trifoliate orange

Potentilla fruticosa	cinquefoil
Ribes aureum*	Missouri currant
Rosa*	
Spiraea thunbergii*	
Syringa*	lilac

Vines:

Anredera cordifolia*	Madeira vine
Clematis**	
Ipomoea alba*	moonflower
Ipomoea quamoclit	cypress-vine
Jasminum*	jasmine
Lonicera*	honeysuckle
Passiflora	passionflower
Phaseolus coccineus	scarlet runner bean
Wisteria*	

Ground covers:

Ajuga reptans	bugle weed
Asarum canadense	wild ginger
Asperula odorata*	sweet woodruff
Ceratostigma plumbaginoides	plumbago
Chrysogonum virginianum	
Hedera helix	English ivy
Liriope	lily turf
Origanum vulgare 'Aureum'	golden creeping oregano
Phalaris	ribbon grass, gardener's garters
Ranunculus repens	creeping buttercup
Stachys byzantina	lamb's ears
Thymus*	thyme
Vinca	

Herbaceous plants for sun:

Achillea*	yarrow
Alcea rosea	hollyhock
Allium	
Artemisia*	wormwood
Aurinia saxatilis	hardy alyssum, basket-of-gold
Asclepias tuberosa	butterfly weed
Aster	
Calendula	pot marigold
Catananche	cupid's dart
Celosia	cockscomb
Centaurea	bachelor's button
Cerastium tomentosum	snow-in-summer
Chrysanthemum leucanthemum	oxeye daisy
Chrsanthemum maximum	Shasta daisy
Cleome	spider flower
Consolida ambigua	larkspur
Coreopsis	tickseed
Cosmos	
Delosperma	
Delphinium	
Dianthus*	pink
Dictamnus	gas plant
Dyssodia	Dahlberg daisy
Echinacea	purple coneflower
Erigeron	fleabane
Eryngium	sea holly
Eschscholzia	California poppy
Eustoma	prairie gentian
Herbs**	

Gaura lindheimeri			*Tagetes**	marigold
Gomphrena	globe amaranth		*Teucrium*	germander
Helianthemum	sun rose, rock rose		*Tropaeolum majus*	nasturtium
Helichrysum	strawflower		*Verbascum*	mullein
Hemerocallis	daylily		*Zauschneria*	California fuchsia
Iris			*Zinnia*	

Gaura lindheimeri

Gomphrena — globe amaranth

Helianthemum — sun rose, rock rose

Helichrysum — strawflower

Hemerocallis — daylily

Iris

*Lavandula** — lavender

Liatris — gayfeather

*Lilium** — lily

Linaria — toadflax

Lunaria annua — money plant

Lythrum — purple loosestrife

Mirabilis — four o'clocks

*Monarda** — beebalm

*Nepeta** — catmint

*Nicotiana** — flowering tobacco

Nigella damascena — love-in-a-mist

Oenothera speciosa — showy primrose

*Paeonia*** — peony

Papaver — poppy

Penstemon — beard-tongue

*Perovskia** — Russian sage

Physostegia — false dragonhead

Portulaca grandiflora — moss rose

Rudbeckia — coneflower, black-eyed Susan

*Salvia** — sage

*Santolina** — lavender cotton

Saponaria — soapwort, bouncing bet

Sedum

Silene — sweet william catchfly

*Tagetes** — marigold

Teucrium — germander

Tropaeolum majus — nasturtium

Verbascum — mullein

Zauschneria — California fuchsia

Zinnia

Herbaceous plants that prefer sun but will bloom in partial shade:

Though most of the spring-flowering bulbs need sun to bloom, they will thrive in the high shade of deciduous trees, blooming and often ripening foliage before tree leaves are fully out.

*Alchemilla** — lady's-mantle

Anemone japonica — windflower

Anemone sylvestris

Aquilegia — columbine

Campanula — bellflower

Geranium

Heuchera — coralbells

Impatiens balsamina — balsam

Lobularia maritima — sweet alyssum

Lupinus — lupine

Lycoris — spider lily, naked lady, surprise lily

Myosotis — forget-me-not

Phlox

Talinum — jewels-of-Opar

Plants that prefer shade to partial shade:

Arum italicum

Aruncus — goatsbeard

Astilbe

*Convallaria** — lily-of-the-valley

Cyclamen

Dark red and white peonies and blue and white iris create a rich tapestry of colors and forms in this garden.

Filipendula	dropwort, meadowsweet
Helleborus	hellebore, Christmas rose, Lenten rose
Hypoestes	polka-dot plant
Lobelia cardinalis	cardinal flower
Mertensia	Virginia bluebell
Primula	primrose
Pulmonaria	lungwort
Stokesia	
Thalictrum	meadow rue
*Viola**	violet, pansy, johnny-jump-up

* denotes fragrant or aromatic flowers or foliage
** some varieties or species fragrant

Marigolds add bright color to the cottage garden and tolerate the heat of summer. The vine growing over the fence is Basella alba 'Rubra', a wonderful substitute for spinach. It is heat tolerant and its red stems are very attractive.

Photos by Elvin McDonald

Useful Addresses

Organizations:

The Cottage Garden
Society
Mrs. P. Carr
15 Faenol Avenue
Abergele, Clywd, LL22
7HT, Great Britain

Heritage Roses Group
c/o Lily Shohan,
Northeast region
coordinator
RD 1, Box 299
Clinton Corners, NY
12514

Heritage Roses Group
Dr. Henry Najat
6365 Wald Road
Monroe, WI 53566

Historical Iris
Preservation Society
c/o Verona Wiekhorst
4855 Santiago Way
Colorado Springs, CO
80917

The Hardy Plant Society
Joanne Walkovic,
Mid-Atlantic group
539 Woodland Avenue
Media, PA 19063

North American Fruit
Explorers
Route 1, Box 94
Chapin, IL 62628
Society for old and
unusual fruits

Nurseries:

Antique Rose Emporium
Route 5, Box 143
Brenham, TX 77833

Appalachian Gardens
Box 82
Waynesboro, PA 17268
Hardy ornamental trees
and shrubs

*Peony 'Coral Charm' combines nicely with the
soft yellow iris. The foliage of peonies enhances
the garden even when the plant is not
in bloom.*

B & D Lilies
330 P Street
Port Townsend, WA
98368

Bluestone Perennials
7211 Middle Ridge Road
Madison, OH 44057

Busse Gardens
Route 2, Box 238
Cokato, MN 55321

Perennials, especially
hostas, daylilies, peonies

Canyon Creek Nursery
3527 Dry Creek Road
Oroville, CA 95965
Perennial seeds

Carroll Gardens
P.O. Box 310
Westminster, MD 21157
Perennials, shrubs, lilies,
roses

Catnip Acres
Christian Street
Oxford, CT 06483-1224
Herbs

Clifford's Perennial &
Vine
Route 2, Box 328
East Troy, WI 53120
Perennials, clematis,
shrubs

Companion Plants
7247 N. Coolville Ridge
Road
Athens, OH 45701
Herbs

Comstock, Ferre and Co.
P.O. Box 125
Wethersfield, CT 06109
General seed catalog

Country Garden
Route 2, Box 455A
Crivitz, WI 54114
Varieties for cutting

C.A. Cruikshank
1015 Mt. Pleasant Road
Toronto, Ontario M4P
2M1
Bulbs, including many
unusual

Daffodil Mart
Route 3, Box 794
Gloucester, VA 23061

De Giorgi Co.
1529 N. Saddle Creek
Road
Omaha, NE 68104
General seed catalog

Far North Gardens
16785 Harrison
Livonia, MI 48154
Primroses and rare flower
seeds

Henry Field Seed &
Nursery Co.
Shenandoah, IA 51602
General seed and plant
catalog

Fox Hill Farm
440 W. Michigan Avenue,
Box 9
Parma, MI 49269

The Fragrant Path
P.O. Box 328
Fort Calhoun, NE 68023
Seeds of fragrant,
old-fashioned plants

Gurney Seed & Nursery
Co.
Yankton, SD 57079
General Seed Catalog

Heirloom Garden Seeds
P.O. Box 138
West Elizabeth, PA
15088-0245
Heirloom and
old-fashioned vegetable
seeds

Heritage Rose Gardens
16831 Mitchell Creek
Drive
Fort Bragg, CA 95437

High Country Rosarium
1717 Downing Street
Denver, CO 80218
Species, shrub and old
garden roses

Historical Roses
1657 W. Jackson Street
Painesville, OH 44077

J.L. Hudson, Seedsman
P.O. Box 1058
Redwood City, CA 94064
Rare seeds from around
the world

Thomas Jefferson Center
for Historic Plants
Monticello
P.O. Box 316
Charlottesville, VA 22901

Johnson's Nursery
Route 5, Box 29J
Ellijay, GA 30540
Fruits for the South

D. Landreth Seed Co.
P.O. Box 6426
Baltimore, MD 21230
General seed catalog

Lawson's Nursery
Route 1, Box 473
Ball Ground, GA 30107
Antique apples

Leuthardt Nurseries
P.O. Box 666
East Moriches, NY 11950
Espaliered fruit trees

Living Tree Centre
P.O. Box 797
Bolinas, CA 94914
Antique apples

Lowe's Own-Root Roses
6 Sheffield Road
Nashua, NJ 03062
Roses grown to order

Makielski Berry Farms &
Nursery
7130 Platt
Ypsilanti, MI 48197
Bush fruits

McClure & Zimmerman
1422 Thorndale
Chicago, IL 60660
Good selection of bulbs

Messelaar Bulb Co.
Box 269
Ipswich, MA 01938

J.E. Miller Nurseries
5060 W. Lake Road
Canandaigua, NY 14424
Fruits, trees and shrubs

Milaegers
4838 Douglas Avenue
Racine, WI 53402-2498
Perennials

Montrose Nursery
P.O. Box 957
Hillsborough, NC 27278
Species cyclamen and
perennials

New York State Fruit
Testing Coop. Ass'n
P.O. Box 462
Geneva, NY 14456

Old Thyme Flower &
Herbal Seed Exchange/B.
Bond
Route 1, Box 124A
Nebraska City, NE 68410

George W. Park Seed Co.
Greenwood, SC
29647-0001

Pickering Nurseries
670 Kingston Road
Pickering, Ontario L1V
1A6

Plants of the Southwest
1812 Second Street
Santa Fe, NM 87501
Southwest natives

Prairie Nursery
P.O. Box 365
Westfield, WI 53964
Prairie plants, seeds,
grasses and wildflowers

Richters
Goodwood, Ontario
LOC 1A0

Roses of Yesterday and
Today
802 Brown's Valley Road
Watsonville, CA
95076-0398

Sandy Mush Herb
Nursery
Route 2, Surrett Cove
Road
Leicester, NC 28748

John Scheepers, Inc.
RD 6, Phillipsburg Road
Middletown, NY 10940
Bulbs

Seed Source/Sharp Plants
Route 2, Box 265B
Asheville, NC 28805
Unusual seeds

Select Seeds
81 Stickney Hill Road
Union, CT 06076
Seeds of old-fashioned
and heirloom plants

Southern Exposure Seed
Exchange
P.O. Box 158
Beaumont, TX 77702
Heirloom plant seeds

Southmeadow Fruit
Gardens
15310 Red Arrow
Highway
Lakeside, MI 49116
Antique varieties of trees
and small fruits

Stokes Seeds
Box 548
Buffalo, NY 14240
Extensive seed catalog

Thompson & Morgan
P.O. Box 1308
Jackson, NJ 08527
Extensive seed catalog

Van Engelen Inc.
Stillbrook Farm
307 Maple Street
Litchfield, CT 06759
Bulbs

Andre Viette Farm and
Nursery
Route 1, Box 16
Fisherville, VA 22939
Perennials

Wayside Gardens
P.O. Box 1
Hodges, SC 29695-0001
Perennials, shrubs

Well-Sweep Herb Farm
317 Mt. Bethel Road
Port Murray, NJ 07865

Photo by Elvin McDonald

Marigolds and basil are two of the heat-tolerant plants in this Park Seed Company display garden.

White Flower Farm
Route 63
Litchfield, CT 06759-0050
Perennials

Worcester Co. Hort. Soc.
30 Tower Hill Road
Boylston, MA 01505
Scion wood of antique
apple varieties for
grafting

A Garden in Winnetka, Illinois